ITQ Level 3

Presentation Software

Using
Microsoft® PowerPoint 2003

Release ITQ48v1

Published by:

CiA Training Ltd
Business & Innovation Centre
Sunderland Enterprise Park
Sunderland SR5 2TH
United Kingdom

Tel: +44 (0)191 549 5002
Fax: +44 (0)191 549 9005

Email: info@ciatraining.co.uk
Web: www.ciatraining.co.uk

ISBN 13: 978 1 86005 764 9

First published 2008

Overview of the Unit

At this level your job role is likely to involve producing technically complex presentations, e.g. including video and sound clips. You need to be able to use the software to produce presentations for education, entertainment or information sharing, including a combination of media, e.g. photos from digital cameras animation and sound.

This unit is called **Presentation Software** and has a unit value of 30 points.

This guide was created using *Microsoft PowerPoint 2003*. It assumes that the program has been correctly and fully installed on your personal computer. Some features described in this guide may not work if the program was not fully installed.

The software includes a comprehensive range of tools for the creation, editing and production of multimedia presentations.

PRESENTATION SOFTWARE UNIT - The guide supporting this optional unit contains exercises covering the following topics:

Master Slides and Style Sheets
Bullet Levels
Title Slide and Notes Master
Background Effects
Creating and Using Templates
Drawing Objects
Inserting Pictures
Charts and Tables
Importing and Exporting Data
Sounds and Movies
Hiding Slides
Summary Slides
Action Buttons and Hyperlinks
Animation Effects
Slide Transitions and Timings
Custom Shows
Recording Macros
Printing Slides and Handouts
Saving in Various Formats

*Visit **www.ciasupport.co.uk** for hints, tips and supplementary information on published CiA products.*

This guide is suitable for:

- Any individual wishing to gain the skills necessary to produce ITQ evidence for this Unit. The user works through the guide from start to finish. Some prior knowledge of *PowerPoint 2003* would be useful, e.g. Level 2.

- Tutor led groups as reinforcement material. It can be used as and when necessary.

Aims and Objectives

- To provide the knowledge and techniques necessary for the attainment of a certificate in this optional unit. After completing the guide the user will be able to:
- Use presentation software efficiently to produce technically complex and interactive presentations that communicate effectively.
- Understand and acquire the skills needed to produce these presentations.

Downloading the Data Files

The data associated with these exercises must be downloaded from our website. Go to: **www.ciatraining.co.uk/data**. Follow the on screen instructions to download the appropriate data files.

By default, the data files will be downloaded to **My Documents\CIA DATA FILES\ITQ Level 3\PowerPoint 2003 Data**.

If you prefer, the data can be supplied on CD at an additional cost. Contact the Sales team at **info@ciatraining.co.uk**.

Important Notes For All Users

The downloadable data accompanying this guide contains files to enable the user to practise new techniques without the need for data entry. Newly created files can be saved to the same location.

Notation Used Throughout This Guide

- Key presses are included within **< >** e.g. <**Enter**> means press the **Enter** key.
- The guide is split into individual exercises. Each exercise consists of a written explanation of the feature, followed by a stepped exercise.

Recommendations

- Work through the exercises in sequence so that one feature is understood before moving on to the next.
- Read the whole of each exercise before starting to work through it. This ensures the understanding of the topic and prevents unnecessary mistakes.

Pre-Assessment Checklist

This checklist is to be used to assess your skills while working through the guide. This is a self assessment process; you judge when you are competent. Before starting a skill set, complete the associated part of the checklist below.

Tick boxes are provided for each feature: **1** indicates you have no knowledge of the feature, **2** indicates some knowledge and **3** indicates full competence. After you've finished working through the skill set, come back to the checklist and complete it again. A skill set is only complete when column **3** is ticked for all exercises included in that skill set.

Tick the Relevant Boxes **1**: No Knowledge **2**: Some Knowledge **3**: Competent

Skill Set	**No**	**Exercise**	**1**	**2**	**3**
1 Preparation	1	Design Considerations			
	2	Styles			
	3	The Slide Master			
	4	Bullet Levels			
	5	Line Spacing and Paragraph Spacing			
	6	Title Master			
	7	Notes Master			
	8	Colour Schemes			
	9	Background Effects			
	10	Creating a Template			
	11	Using a Template			
	12	Slide Design and Setup			
	13	Producing Evidence			
2 Images & Drawn Objects	15	Text Boxes and Drawing Objects			
	16	Object Backgrounds			
	17	Inserting WordArt			
	18	Inserting Clip Art			
	19	Inserting Animated Clips			
	20	Inserting a Picture from a File			
3 Charts, Tables, Importing & Linking	22	Organisation Charts			
	23	Formatting Organisation Charts			
	24	Inserting a Table			
	25	Inserting Charts			

Section	Exercise	Topic			
3 Charts, Tables, Importing & Linking Continued	26	Formatting Charts			
	27	Importing a Chart			
	28	Linking			
	29	Modifying Linked Data			
4 Multimedia	31	Inserting Sounds			
	32	Inserting Movies			
	33	Video Editing			
	34	Introducing Animation			
	35	Animation Sequences			
	36	Animating Charts			
5 Slide Shows	38	Inserting Slides			
	39	Hiding Slides			
	40	Custom Shows			
	41	Running a Custom Show			
	42	Action Buttons			
	43	Editing an Action Button			
	44	Using Hyperlinks in Slides			
	45	Applying Transitions			
	46	Applying Timings			
	47	Setting up a Slide Show			
6 Macros	49	Recording a Macro			
	50	Running a Macro			
	51	Multiple Action Macros			
	52	Assigning a Macro			
7 Finishing and Printing	54	Adding Speaker's Notes			
	55	Start and End Slides			
	56	Creating a Summary Slide			
	57	Perfecting Your Presentation			
	58	Reviewing			
	59	Compare and Merge			
	60	Printing Slides and Presentations			
	61	Package for CD			
	62	Publishing to the Web			

SKILL SET 1 PREPARATION **9**
1 - DESIGN CONSIDERATIONS 10
2 - STYLES 11
3 - THE SLIDE MASTER 12
4 - BULLET LEVELS 14
5 - LINE SPACING AND PARAGRAPH SPACING 15
6 - TITLE MASTER 16
7 - NOTES MASTER 17
8 - COLOUR SCHEMES 18
9 - BACKGROUND EFFECTS 20
10 - CREATING A TEMPLATE 22
11 - USING A TEMPLATE 23
12 - SLIDE DESIGN AND SETUP 25
13 - PRODUCING EVIDENCE 26
14 - DEVELOP YOUR SKILLS 28
SUMMARY: PREPARATION 29
SKILL SET 2 IMAGES & DRAWN OBJECTS **30**
15 - TEXT BOXES AND DRAWING OBJECTS 31
16 - OBJECT BACKGROUNDS 32
17 - INSERTING WORDART 34
18 - INSERTING CLIP ART 36
19 - INSERTING ANIMATED CLIPS 37
20 - INSERTING A PICTURE FROM A FILE 38
21 - DEVELOP YOUR SKILLS 40
SUMMARY: IMAGES AND DRAWN OBJECTS 42
SKILL SET 3 CHARTS, TABLES, IMPORTING & LINKING **43**
22 - ORGANISATION CHARTS 44
23 - FORMATTING ORGANISATION CHARTS 46
24 - INSERTING A TABLE 48
25 - INSERTING CHARTS 50
26 - FORMATTING CHARTS 51
27 - IMPORTING A CHART 53
28 - LINKING 54
29 - MODIFYING LINKED DATA 56
30 - DEVELOP YOUR SKILLS 58
SUMMARY - CHARTS, TABLES, IMPORTING & LINKING 61
SKILL SET 4 MULTIMEDIA **62**
31 - INSERTING SOUNDS 63
32 - INSERTING MOVIES 65
33 - VIDEO EDITING 67
34 - INTRODUCING ANIMATION 69
35 - ANIMATION SEQUENCES 70
36 - ANIMATING CHARTS 72
37 - DEVELOP YOUR SKILLS 73
SUMMARY: MULTIMEDIA 75

SKILL SET 5 SLIDE SHOWS **76**
38 - Inserting Slides 77
39 - Hiding Slides 79
40 - Custom Shows 80
41 - Running a Custom Show 82
42 - Action Buttons 83
43 - Editing an Action Button 86
44 - Using Hyperlinks in Slides 87
45 - Applying Transitions 90
46 - Applying Timings 93
47 - Setting up a Slide Show 95
48 - Develop Your Skills 97
Summary: Slide Shows 100
SKILL SET 6 MACROS **101**
49 - Recording a Macro 102
50 - Running a Macro 103
51 - Multiple Action Macros 104
52 - Assigning a Macro 105
53 - Develop Your Skills 108
Summary: Macros 110
SKILL SET 7 FINISHING AND PRINTING **111**
54 - Adding Speaker's Notes 112
55 - Start and End Slides 113
56 - Creating a Summary Slide 114
57 - Perfecting Your Presentation 115
58 - Reviewing 117
59 - Compare and Merge 119
60 - Printing Slides and Presentations 121
61 - Package for CD 123
62 - Publishing to the Web 123
63 - Develop Your Skills 127
Summary: Finishing and Printing 128
EVIDENCE REQUIREMENTS **129**
PRESENTATION SOFTWARE LEVEL 3 CHECKLIST **131**
GLOSSARY **132**
INDEX **134**
OTHER PRODUCTS FROM CIA TRAINING **136**

Skill Set 1

Preparation

By the end of this Skill Set you should be able to:

Appreciate Design Considerations
Set up Master Slides
Use Different Bullet Levels
Change Line and Paragraph Spacing
Apply Background Effects and Colour Schemes
Create a Template
Use a Template
Change Slide Design and Setup
Produce Evidence

Exercise 1 - Design Considerations

PowerPoint is a powerful presentation graphics application, which allows impressive presentations to be produced with ease. Presentations can be viewed on screen, on an overhead projector, on 35mm slides, or as web pages.

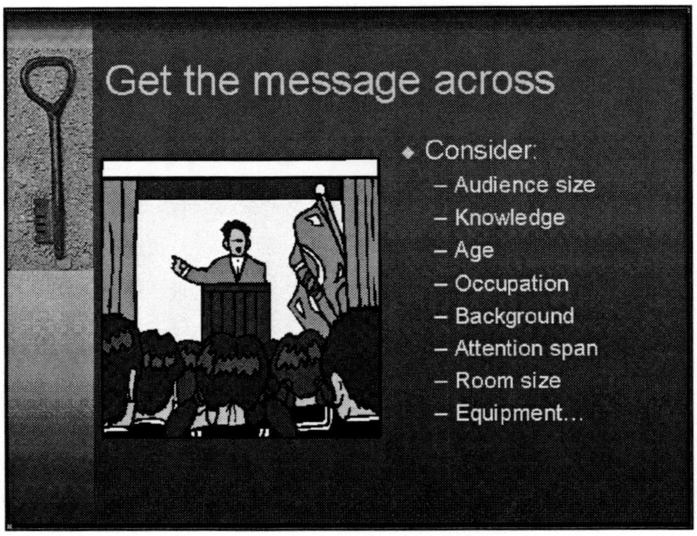

Whilst this guide describes techniques needed to produce and run successful presentations, some thought should always be given to the target audience. Consider how to put your message across: the tone will need to be different for each audience, e.g. it would not be appropriate to deliver a presentation created for children to a business audience, or vice versa. You should also be aware of the level of knowledge the audience has of the subject and pitch the presentation accordingly. Too much explanation of areas with which the audience is familiar may cause them to lose interest. Likewise, too little explanation for an audience with little or no subject knowledge may have the same effect. Consider too the cultural background of the audience and make the presentation fit.

Practical considerations are also important. How big is the audience? How big is the room in which the presentation is to be delivered? You may need a projector and a microphone in a large room. Things like background colour and text legibility become more important in these circumstances.

Plan the length of the presentation appropriately. How much time is available? It may be necessary to create a long or short version of the slide show. Make sure the presentation makes sense - that the slides run in a logical manner. Set the slide timings appropriately - allow enough time to get the points across, but don't ramble or you may lose the attention of the audience.

Visual impact is almost everything in a presentation. You should be aware of the value of using pictures rather than too much text and charts rather than rows of figures. At the same time, don't use too many different background colours or effects; a consistent design scheme makes the message much clearer.

These aesthetic, practical and ethical considerations should be at the forefront when designing any presentation.

Exercise 2 - Styles

As part of the requirements for this Unit you will have to produce a **Slide Master**, to be used in creating presentations. One of the main defining characteristics of any master slide is the font styles. Different parts of slide content may be assigned different styles, e.g. title style, first level text style, and these will then be used consistently throughout the presentation and so achieve a coherent appearance. The various parameters which can define a style are shown in the example below:

Style Name	Font	Line Spacing	Paragraph Spacing	Size	Colour	Alignment	Emphasis
Title Style	***Arial***	***1.25 lines***	***Before 0.3 lines after 0.3 lines***	***32pt***	***Red***	***Left***	***Shadow***

Not all parameters will be defined for every style.

A list defining all the styles to be used in a presentation is sometimes referred to as a **Style Sheet**, and some organisations will have a fixed style sheet which must be used in all presentations.

It is often a good idea to save the fonts which are used in a presentation with the presentation itself. Then if the presentation is opened on a different computer which perhaps does not have the particular fonts installed, it will still be displayed correctly.

Activity:

1. Start a new *PowerPoint* presentation containing a **Title Slide** with no data.

2. Select **Tools | Options** and make sure the **Save** tab is displayed.

3. Select the options to **Embed True Type fonts** and **Embed all characters**.

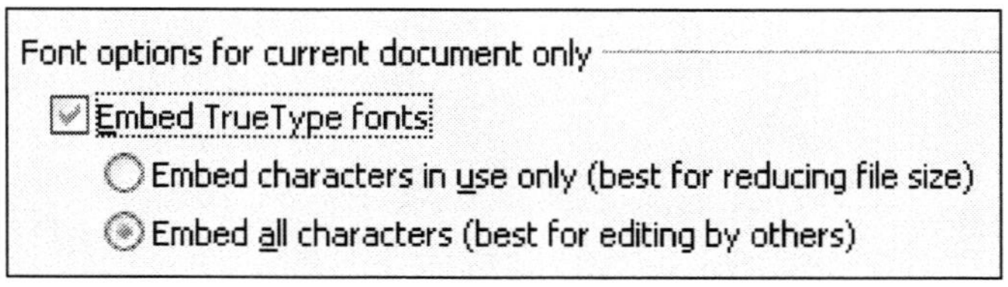

4. Click **OK** to activate this feature.

5. Leave the presentation open.

Exercise 3 - The Slide Master

Master pages contain text or graphics that are to be used on every page of a presentation. There are four master pages: **Slide**, **Title**, **Handout** and **Notes**.

The **Slide Master** allows uniform text or graphics to be added to every slide. A coloured or themed background may also be added. This will create a consistent look to the presentation.

The **Slide Master** will be created using the specifications from the **style sheet** shown in **Exercise 2**. Some of the formatting specifications will be applied in another section of the guide.

Activity:

1. Ensure your presentation has a **Title Slide** with no data. Select **View | Master | Slide Master**. The **Slide Master** is now shown.

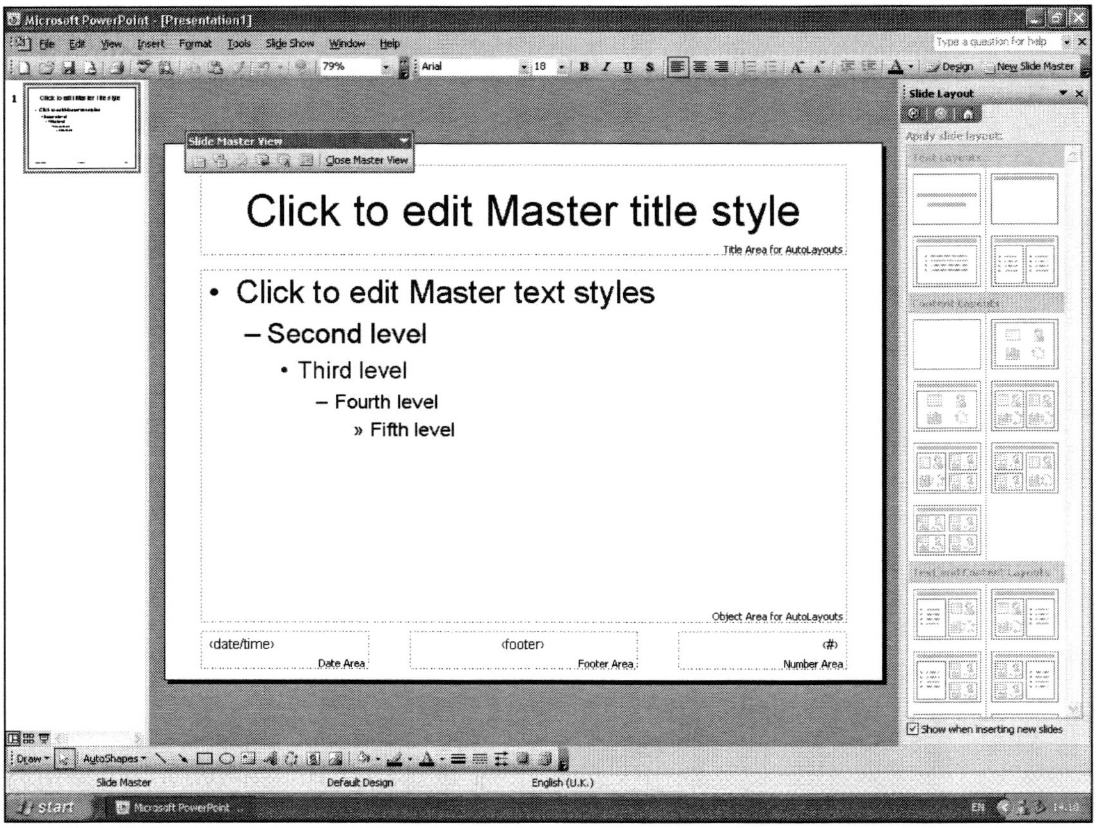

> ***Note:*** *Any changes made in this view will affect the whole presentation and anything put on to this slide will appear on every slide.*

2. Close the **Task Pane** on the right and click on the text **Click to edit Master title style**.

3. From the **Font** drop down list, 

, on the **Formatting** toolbar, select the **Arial Rounded MT Bold** font (use an alternative if this is unavailable).

4. Change the size to **48pt**.

5. Select the second text box: **Click to edit Master text styles**.

6. Click on the top bullet's text and select the font **Arial Rounded MT Bold** but leave the font size as **32pt**.

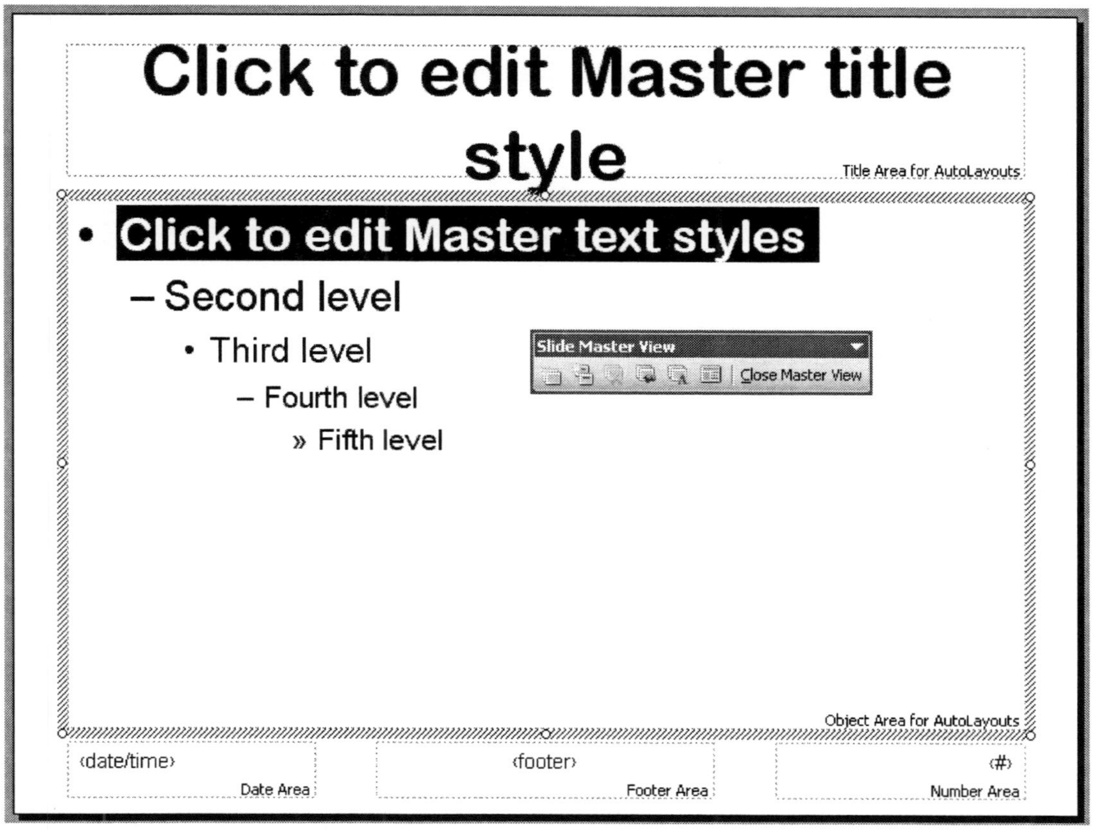

7. Leave the **Slide Master** open.

Exercise 4 - Bullet Levels

Bullets are used to emphasise points in a slide. They can have many different types of symbols. In **Slide Master View** there are several levels of bulleted text available. This allows minor details to be made about major points. By default the bullet levels use the same style of font, etc. but the style can be changed for each level.

> ***Note:*** *In PowerPoint 2003 it is not possible to create one type of style based on another, or to specify that one style automatically follows another. The software automatically adjusts the styles.*

Activity:

1. The **Slide Master** should still be open. Notice that there are **5** bullet levels available.

2. Click in the **Second level** bullet text and change the font to **Arial Rounded MT Bold**. Apply an **italic** effect. Leave the font size the same.

3. To change the bullet character for the second level bullet, make sure the cursor is within the bullet text. Select **Format | Bullets and Numbering** and select the third style on the bottom row of the dialog box.

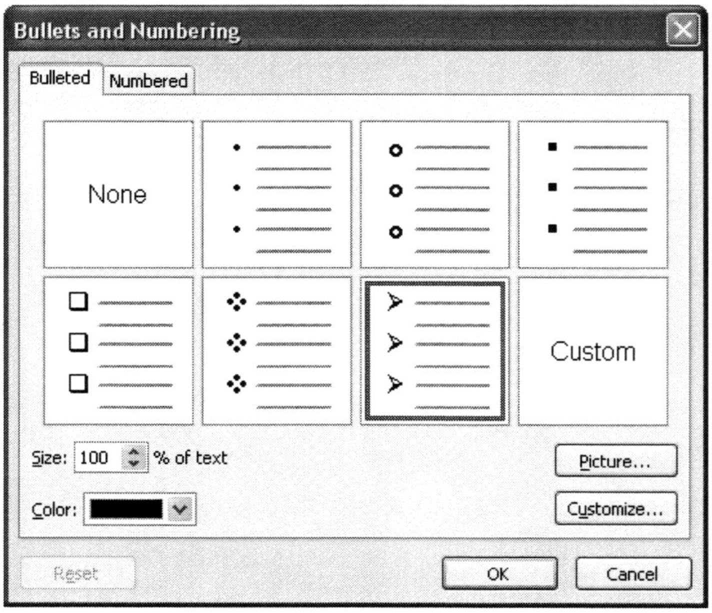

4. Click **OK** to apply the new bullet character.

5. Click in the **Third level** bullet text and change the font to **Arial Rounded MT Bold**, leave the size as **24pt**.

6. Display the **Bullets and Numbering** dialog box and ensure the bullet character is the first style (not **None**) on the top row of the dialog box.

7. Leave the **Slide Master** open and move on to the next exercise.

Exercise 5 - Line Spacing and Paragraph Spacing

Line spacing and paragraph spacing can also be changed on the **Slide Master**, which means it alters all of the slides.

Activity:

1. The **Slide Master** should still be open. Click on the first level bullet (**Click to edit Master text styles**), select **Format | Line Spacing**.

2. Change the **Line spacing** to **1.25 Lines**.

3. Change **Before paragraph** to **0.3 Lines**.

4. Change **After paragraph** to **0.2 Lines**.

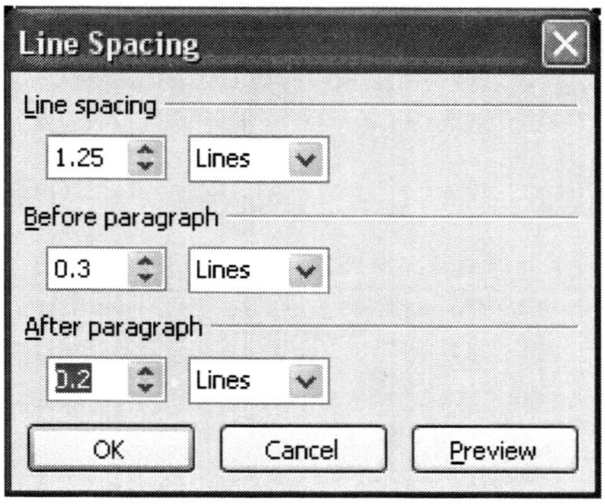

5. Click **OK**.

6. Click on the second level bullet, select **Format | Line Spacing**.

7. Change the **Line spacing** to **1.15 Lines**.

8. Change **After paragraph** to **0.2 Lines**, click **OK**.

9. Click on the third level bullet and change the **Line spacing** to **1.1**.

10. Change **After paragraph** to **0.2 Lines**.

11. Click **OK**.

12. Leave the **Slide Master** open.

Exercise 6 - Title Master

Unlike the **Slide Master**, the **Title Master** only affects the **Title Slide**. It allows you to create a different look for your opening slide in your presentation, or for any slides that may be used to introduce a new section in the presentation.

The **Slide Master** should be created first before changing the **Title Master**, as any formatting which is changed on the **Slide Master** also changes the **Title Master**.

Activity:

1. The **Slide Master** should still be open, click the **Insert New Title Master** button, , on the **Slide Master View** toolbar. The **Title Master** is now shown.

2. Click on the text **Click to edit Master title style** and change the font to **Copperplate Gothic Bold** (use an alternative if this is unavailable).

3. Change the font size to **50pt** (you will need to type the size into the box).

4. Click on the text **Click to edit Master subtitle style** and change the font to **Copperplate Gothic Bold**.

5. Change the font size to **36pt**.

6. Save the presentation as **Master** (see Page 4 - **Downloading the Data Files** for the location of the supplied data files) and leave it open.

Exercise 7 - Notes Master

The **Notes Master**, like the **Slide Master**, allows uniform text or graphics to be added to the notes page of every slide.

Each slide in a presentation has a **Notes Page**, where you can create notes for yourself to help you remember key points during a presentation.

Any items which you include on the **Notes Master** will appear on every notes page in your presentation.

Activity:

1. The **Title Master** should still be open, select **View | Master | Notes Master**. The **Notes Master** is shown (the example below is viewed at **41%**).

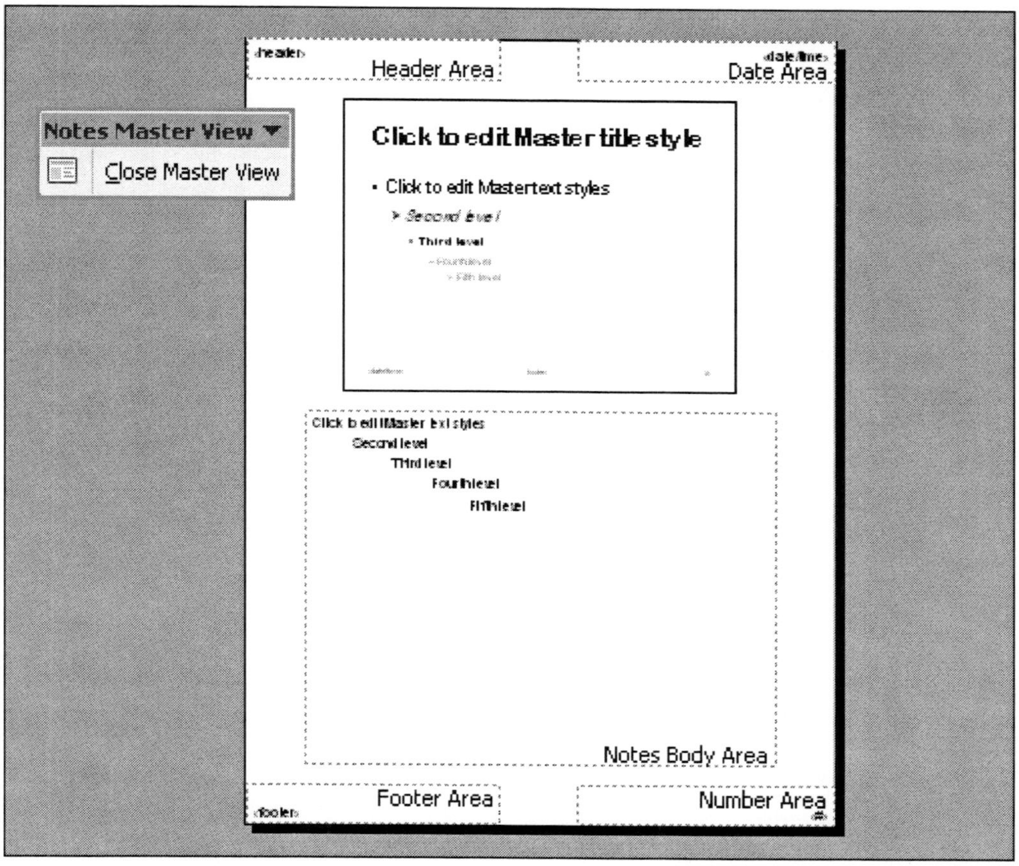

2. Click on the text **Click to edit Master text styles** at the top of the lower text box and change the font to **Times New Roman**, zooming in if necessary.

3. Change the size to **14pt**.

4. Close the **Notes Master**, by clicking, Close Master View.

5. Save the presentation and close it.

Exercise 8 - Colour Schemes

It is normal practice to use **colour schemes** in slides. A colour scheme is a set of predetermined colours that is applied to specific areas of a slide. When a presentation is first created, a particular colour scheme is applied by default, but this scheme can be changed or a new one selected. Standard colour schemes are designed to compliment the design template of the presentation, but individual colours within a scheme can be amended.

Activity:

1. Open the presentation **CIA Seminar** from the data supplied with this guide.

2. This presentation has a design template of **Artsy** applied. Look at the **Slides Pane** at the left of the screen to see the consistent appearance of each slide.

3. To change the colour scheme select **Format | Slide Design** and from the **Task Pane** click Color Schemes. The scheme at the top left is the default scheme for this design.

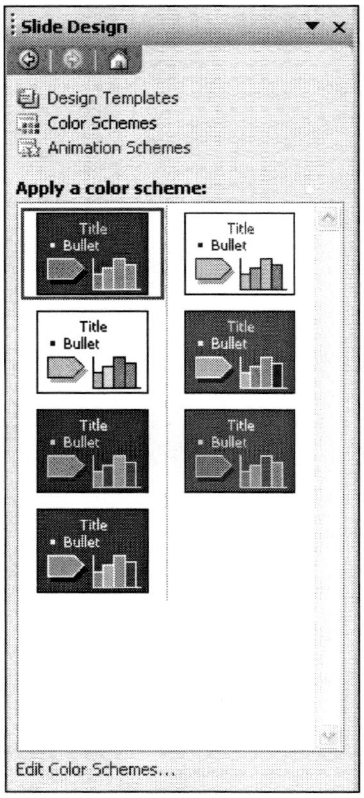

4. Click on the fifth scheme (with the dark red background) and all slides in the presentation change to the new colour scheme. The design template remains the same.

> ***Note:*** *The new scheme could be applied to the currently selected slide only by selecting the* ***Apply to Selected Slides*** *option from the drop down arrow. To maintain a consistent look to the presentation however it is recommended that all slides be changed.*

5. To customise the scheme click **Edit Color Schemes** at the bottom of the **Task Pane**. The dialog box now shows the individual colours that make up the current colour scheme.

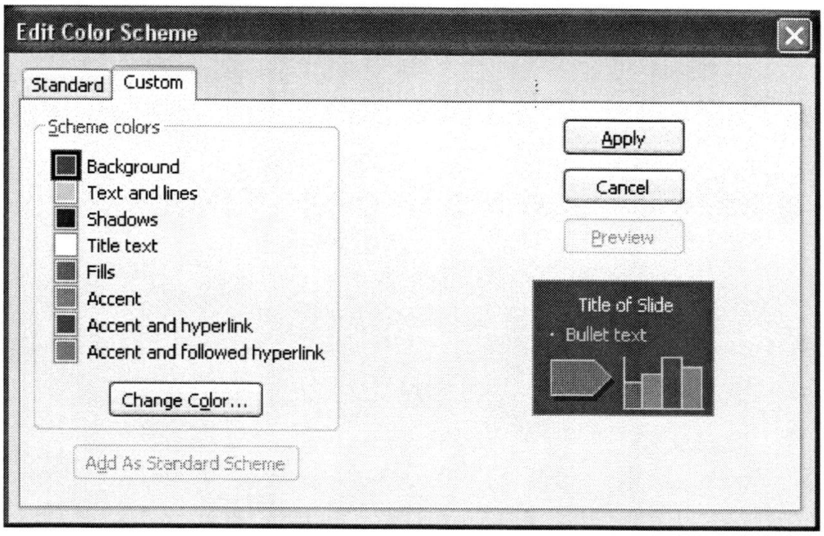

6. Select the small colour box for **Title text** and click **Change Color**. A colour chart is displayed showing the current colour for this feature.

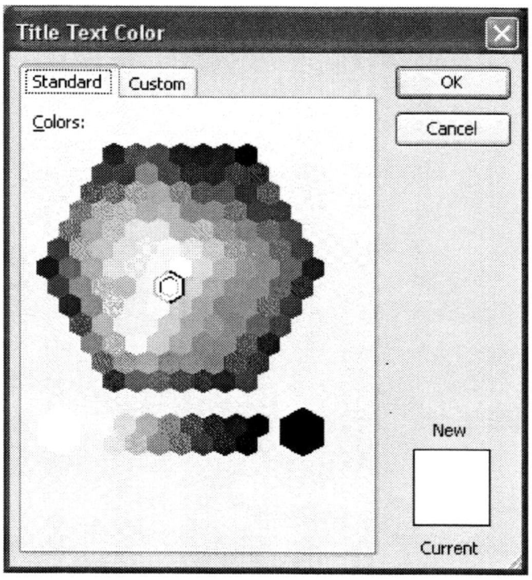

7. Select a pale pink colour from the chart and click **OK**.

8. The new colour for **Title text** is shown in the dialog box. Click **Apply** to change it on all of the slides.

9. Leave the presentation open.

Exercise 9 - Background Effects

As well as colour changes, various other effects can be applied to the overall slide background. These can be applied to slides with or without design templates already in place, and generally they are more effective when applied to less cluttered slide designs. Effects that can be added are colour gradients, textures, patterns and pictures.

Activity:

1. The **CiA Seminar** presentation should already be open from the previous exercise, if not open it.

2. Select **Format | Background**.

3. To apply a background effect, click on the arrow of the drop down box to change the background colour and then select **Fill Effects**. Make sure the **Gradient** tab is selected.

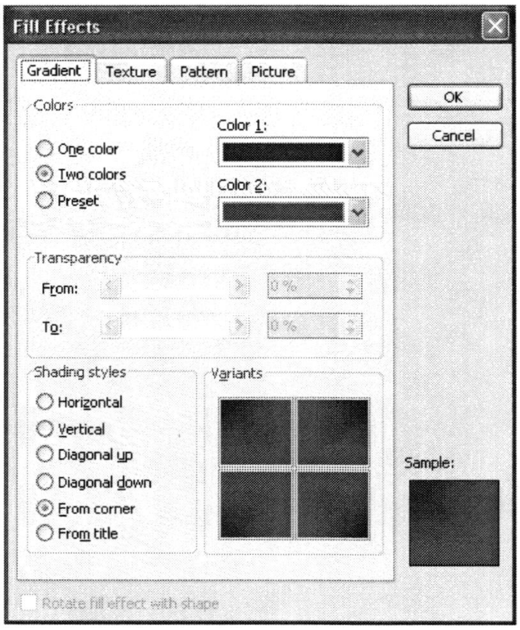

4. Colour gradients can be created from any two colours (**Color 1** and **Color 2**) or selected from an existing list. Click **Preset** and select **Late Sunset** from the drop down list.

5. Click **OK** then **Apply to All**.

> ***Note:*** *Only the background of the slides changes. This can cause problems if a new background causes the content of the slides to be less visible, e.g. if a light background is applied behind light coloured text. Some trial and error may be involved to find a suitable effect.*

6. Select **Format | Background**, click the drop down arrow and select **Fill Effects**. This time select the **Texture** tab.

7. Click on each available texture. The name of the texture is displayed underneath. Select **Brown marble**.

8. Click **OK** then **Apply to All**.

9. Display the **Fill Effects** dialog box again and select the **Pattern** tab.

10. A selection of patterns is available based on a **Foreground** and **Background** colour (these can be changed). Select a reasonably dark pattern and click **OK**.

11. Click **Apply to All** to see the effect.

12. Display the **Fill Effects** dialog box again and select the **Picture** tab.

13. Any picture stored on the computer can be used as a background. Click **Select Picture** and ensure the location of the supplied data files is in the **Look in** box.

14. Select the **ostrich** file and click **Insert**. Select **OK** at the **Fill Effects** dialog box.

15. Select the option to **Omit background graphics from master** from the **Background** dialog box.

16. Click **Apply to All**.

> ***Note:*** *Pictures can be effective backgrounds and add an exclusive appearance to a presentation, but care must be taken. Pictures are more likely to distract attention from the slide contents.*

17. Save the presentation as **Big Bird** and close it.

Exercise 10 - Creating a Template

Having spent considerable time and effort creating a suitable appearance for your presentation, you may wish to apply the same look to subsequent slide shows. Any layout can be saved as a **template** and then used as a basis for further presentations. This is particularly relevant for organisations, which often want a consistent corporate image for all their presentations.

Activity:

1. Open the presentation **Master** saved in **Exercise 6**. If the presentation does not open in **Slide Master View**, select **View | Master | Slide Master** and select the **Slide Master** (**1**) from the top of the pane at the left of the screen.

2. Select **Format | Background** and display the **Fill Effects** dialog box.

3. Select the **Texture** tab then scroll down and select the texture **Canvas**. Click **OK** then **Apply to All**.

4. Click in the **Master title style** box and change the font to **italic**, the font colour to dark blue and the alignment to **Align Left**.

5. Click on the text **Click to edit Master text styles** and change the font colour to red.

6. Click on the **Second level bullet** and change the font colour to dark green.

7. Click on the **Third level bullet** and change the font colour to dark green.

8. Click on the **Title Master (2)** in the pane at the left and click on the text **Click to edit Master title style**. Click the **Shadow** button, S, on the **Formatting** toolbar.

9. Click on the text, **Click to edit Master subtitle style**, apply a shadow effect.

10. Close **Master View**. The layout of the slide is now ready to be saved as a template so that it can be easily applied to other presentations. Select **File | Save As**.

11. In the **Save As** dialog box, in the **File name** area, type **Example**.

12. From **Save as type**, select **Design Template (*.pot)**. When this file type is selected the **Save in** box will automatically show **Templates**, the location of the existing *PowerPoint* templates. Click the **Save** button, Save.

> ***Note:*** *Templates could be stored in any location but would not automatically be available within PowerPoint.*

13. Select **File | Close** to close the presentation.

Exercise 11 - Using a Template

Once a template has been saved it can be used to set the appearance of future presentations. New presentations can be started with the design template or existing slides can be converted.

Activity:

1. Select **File | New** and from the **New Presentation Task Pane** click  under **Templates**. Because the **Example** template created in the last exercise was saved in the **Templates** folder, it now appears as an option under the **General** tab.

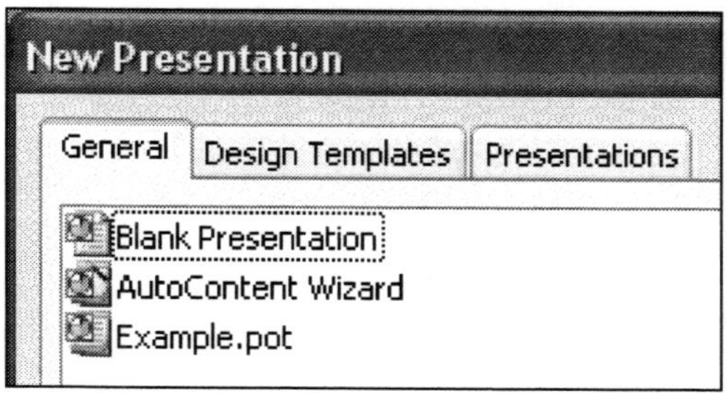

Different templates may be shown on your computer

2. Select **Example.pot**, click **OK**. In **Normal View** on the blank title slide enter **Example** as the title text and your organisation name as the subtitle text.

3. Click  , to insert a new slide and select the **Title and Text** layout from the **Task Pane**.

4. Click to add a title of **Contents** and add four bulleted text lines of **Introduction**, **The Way Forward**, **History** and **Background**. Notice that all of the features defined when creating the template are being applied here, i.e. background, title style, and bullet style.

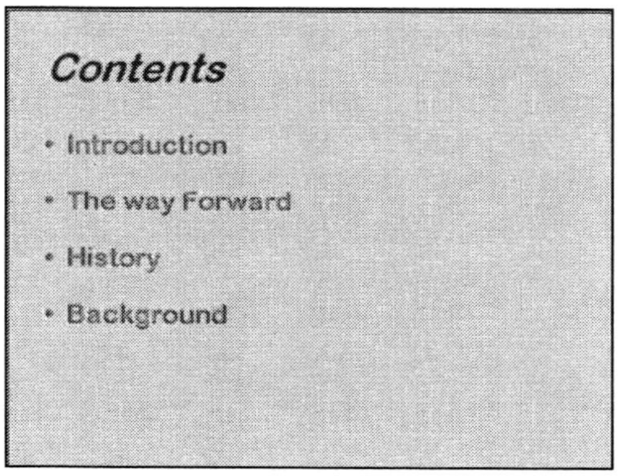

5. Close the new presentation <u>without</u> saving and open the presentation **IT Training** from the supplied data files.

6. To apply the layout and colours of the template select **Format | Slide Design**. Click **Browse** at the bottom of the **Task Pane** and the **Apply Design Template** dialog box is shown.

7. The new template **Example** will now be available from this list. Select it and click **Apply**.

8. All features of the layout are applied to all of the slides in the presentation. Display slide **3** to see the effect more clearly.

9. All the bullets are displayed at level one, to change from level one to level two, click anywhere in the text, • 1 – no knowledge of the subject.

10. Display the **Outlining** toolbar and click the **Demote** button, . The text becomes second level and the bullet changes to an arrow, which was defined earlier for the second level.

***Note:** If the **Outlining** toolbar is not displayed, select **View | Toolbars | Outlining**.*

11. Change bullet **2** and bullet **3** list items to second level bullets in the same way.

12. Display slide **6**, change the second list item to a second level bullet.

13. Click anywhere in the text **Hopefully you should be able to tick box 3 for all subjects** and click the **Demote** button **twice**. The text becomes a third level bullet.

14. The third level text is not correct. Change the text back to a second level bullet by clicking the **Promote** button, , once.

15. Save the presentation as **IT Training Modified** and leave it open.

16. To delete a template, select **Browse** from the **Slide Design** task pane. Right click on the **Example** template.

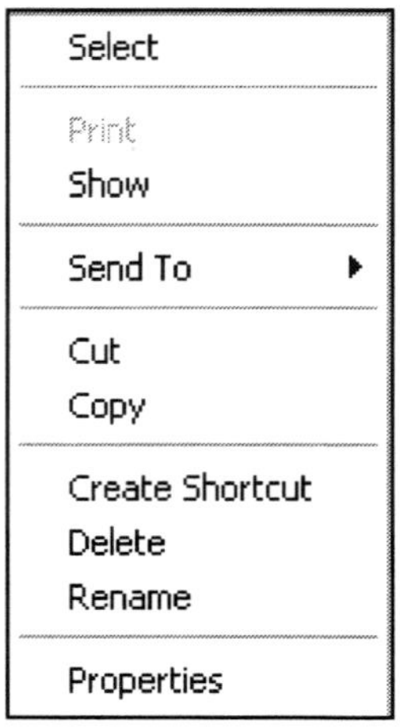

17. Select **Delete** from the shortcut menu. If you click **Yes** at the confirmation dialog box the template will be deleted, in this instance click **No**.

18. Close the **Apply Design Template** dialog box, but leave the presentation open.

Exercise 12 - Slide Design and Setup

The design chosen when the presentation was first created can be changed at any time. The slide setup, e.g. the slide size and orientation may be changed, as well as the orientation of the **Notes Pages**, **Handouts** and **Outlines**.

Activity:

1. In **Normal View**, from the **Slide Design** task pane, click on the **Capsules** design to apply it.
2. The slide design will change to **Capsules** (it may take a little while for all of the colours, etc. to be updated). Look at the **Slides** pane to check that the design of all the slides has been changed.
3. Select **File | Page Setup**.
4. To see the slides with different orientation applied, select **Portrait** from the **Slides** area.

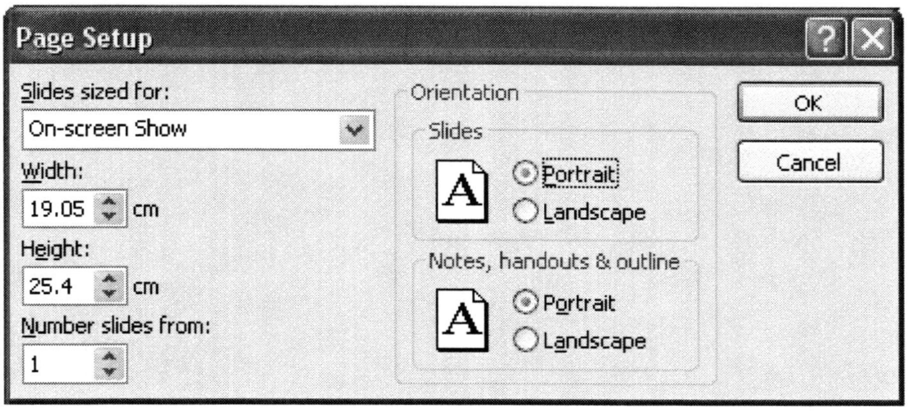

5. Click **OK**. To change the width and height of each slide, select **File | Page Setup**, change the slide **Width** to **17cm** and slide **Height** to **23 cm**, click **OK**.
6. To change the presentation back to its original settings, select **File | Page Setup**, from the **Slides sized for** drop down list select **On-screen Show**, select **Landscape** from the **Slides** area and then click **OK**.
7. Save the presentation as **Training** and close it.

Exercise 13 - Producing Evidence

As a requirement for this unit, you may need to make many printouts of your templates, slides, dialog boxes, etc. This is to produce evidence that you have created the objects, or changed the settings necessary to satisfy the various criteria that will be requested. This exercise will help you to understand the type of evidence that is required and the revision exercises allow you to practise producing evidence.

Activity:

1. Select **File | New** and click On my computer... in the **Task Pane**. The **Example** template is shown in the list.

2. To make a copy of what you can see on the screen (this is called a **screen print** or **screen dump**), press the **Print Screen** key at the top right of the keyboard.

3. Close the dialog box.

Note: *The image is copied to the Windows* ***Clipboard****.*

4. Open *Microsoft Word*.

5. To paste the image on to the blank page, click the **Paste** button, . The page now shows the screen print.

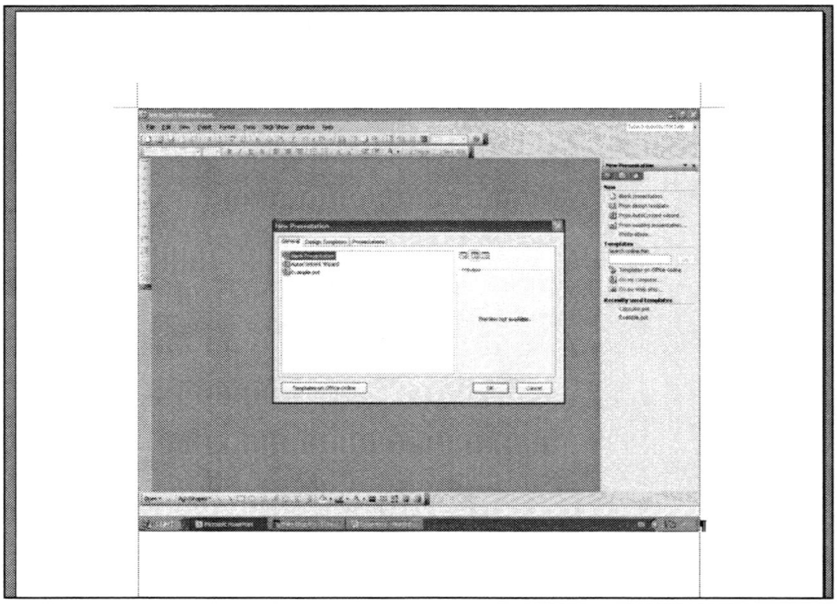

6. Beneath the image, type **Evidence of Master Slide saved as a template**.

Note: *The key press* <***Alt Print Screen***> *captures the active dialog box rather than the full screen.*

7. Switch back to *PowerPoint*. Now a screen print of the **Slide Master** is required.

8. Select **File | Open** select the **Example** template found on **C:\Documents and Settings*username*\Application Data\Microsoft\Templates**, and click **Open**.

> ***Note:*** *In Windows XP, the* ***Application Data*** *folder may be hidden. If you can't find it, open* ***My Computer*** *and select* ***Tools | Folder Options*** *and the* ***View*** *tab. Select* ***Show hidden files and folders*** *and click* ***OK***.

9. Close the **Task Pane** and view the **Slide Master**. You have to provide evidence of styles and formatting used. Click the title box, delete the text and type **Arial Rounded MT Bold italic 48 left**.

10. Click on the first level bullet and type, **Arial Rounded MT Bold 32 left**. Type **Arial Rounded MT Bold italic 28 left** for level 2 and **Arial Rounded MT Bold 24 left** for level 3. Click away from the slide to reveal the background.

11. Press <**Print Screen**> and paste the screen dump in to the new *Word* document beneath the first.

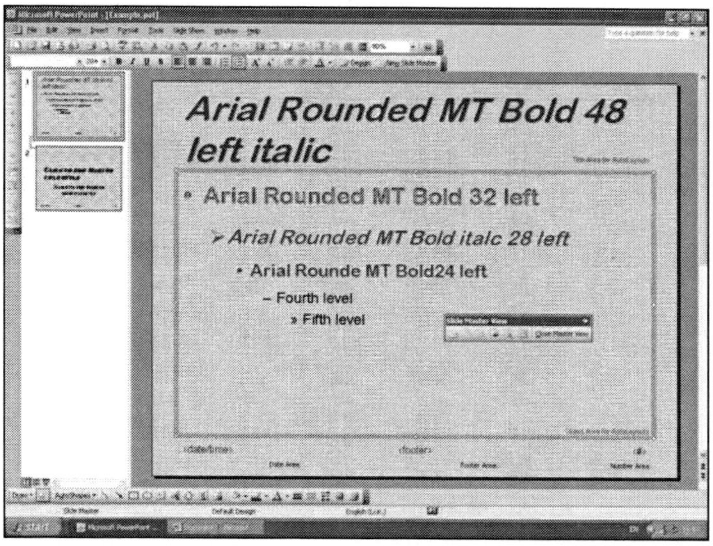

12. Enter **Evidence of Slide Master slides** beneath the image and then switch back to *PowerPoint*.

13. View the **Title Master**, repeat steps **9** to **12**, inserting the relevant font styles and formatting applied (it may be necessary to start a new page).

14. Repeat the steps to produce evidence of the **Notes Master** styles.

15. To obtain a printout, click the **Print** button, , in *Word*.

16. Save the document as **Evidence** and close it. This is to be used to generate evidence as you work through the general exercises. Close *Word*.

17. Close the **Example** template without saving.

Exercise 14 - Develop Your Skills

The revision exercises in this guide allow you to practise producing a task and evidence, using the following scenario:

You are a member of a Promoting and Planning Team. Your College is concerned about the gender split in students and the college image. The College wants to promote widening adult participation in learning, particularly to the female population. Your team has been asked carry out an analysis of the region's population and job opportunities, to come up with new ideas and initiatives, which will take the college forward. You are to prepare a presentation to be shown to all College staff.

1. To set up the master slides which will create a new template, create a new presentation and add a **Title Slide** with no data. View the **Slide Master** and apply the design template **Edge**, to create a custom background.

2. Amend the **Slide Master** applying the following features:
    - Background, texture **Bouquet**
    - Title style, left align, **Rockwell Extra Bold**, **Shadow** effect, size **40pt**, colour **purple**
    - Master text style, **Book Antiqua**, **32pt**, **bold**, colour **blue**, paragraph spacing, before **0.2 lines**, after **0.05 lines**
    - Second level, **Rockwell Condensed**, **28pt**, colour **purple**, paragraph spacing, before **0.2 lines**, after **0.1 lines**

3. Create the **Title Master** applying the following additional features:
    - Title style, change the size to **50pt**
    - Subtitle style, change the alignment to **centre** and the font size to **32pt**.

4. Create a **Notes Master** applying the following features:
    - Master text style, **Broadway**, **14pt**, **blue**.

5. Create a screen print of the screens showing the **Slide Master**, **Title Master**, and **Notes Master**.

6. Paste into a new *Word* document with suitable captions. Enter text below each image with details of the font styles used on that master slide.

7. Use **Tools | Options** to apply the **Embed Fonts** option as described in Exercise 2. Create a screen print of the dialog box showing the relevant settings and paste into the *Word* document.

8. Save the presentation as a **Design Template** with the file name **Exercise1**.

9. Create a screen print of the *PowerPoint* window showing the title bar (**Exercise1.pot**). Create a screen print of the **Task Pane** showing **Exercise1** as a template, paste both images into the *Word* document, add captions.

10. Save the *Word* document as **Revision Evidence** and close it. Close all open presentations.

Summary: Preparation

Producing Evidence

To achieve an ITQ you must prove that you have all of the skills mentioned in these summary pages. You can provide evidence of your competence in several ways:

- A file can be saved and submitted. You can create a **screen print**, which shows exactly what you see on the computer screen, pasted into a document and submitted. This is referred to as Examination of product (EP)
- A process can be seen by an expert witness and a signed document produced. Examination of witness testimony (EWT)
- Observation of candidate (O)
- Examination of case history (ECH)
- Examination of personal statement (EPS)
- Examination of written answers to questions (EWA)
- Questioning of candidate (QC)
- Questioning of witness (QW)
- Professional discussion (PD)
- Vocationally Related Qualification unit (VRQ)

Before submitting your work for assessment, make sure you have gathered sufficient evidence for each item on the Level 3 Evidence Checklist. A copy of the checklist is at the back of this guide.

Your ITQ evidence must demonstrate the following skills:

- Convert files to another suitable format, where necessary
- Check that structure, style and formatting are used to communicate effectively
- Format technically complex and interactive presentations using appropriate tools and techniques. For example: creating a master slide to format consistently; using different formats in each section and creating different slide transitions.

You need to know and understand:

- How to produce information that communicates effectively, by structuring the content to take account of different contexts and audience needs
- How to produce technically complex and interactive presentations. Technically complex and interactive presentations need to be produced using time-line based tools and may include sound and moving images.

Read through the exercises in this Skill Set to give you some ideas of how you could demonstrate these skills.

Skill Set 2

Images & Drawn Objects

By the end of this Skill Set you should be able to:

Insert Text Boxes
Draw Objects
Format Objects
Insert WordArt
Insert Animated Clip Art and Pictures from File

Exercise 15 - Text Boxes and Drawing Objects

The **Drawing** toolbar allows drawings and text boxes to be placed directly on to a slide. The **Drawing** toolbar can only be displayed in **Normal**, **Slide**, **Outline** and **Notes Pages View**. The buttons are:

Draw	Select Objects	AutoShapes
Line	Arrow	Rectangle
Oval	Text box	Insert WordArt
Diagram or Chart	Insert Clip Art	Insert Picture
Fill Color	Line Color	Font Color
Line Style	Dash Style	Arrow Style
Shadow	3D	

Objects can be drawn by clicking on the appropriate button and then clicking and dragging on the slide. All objects have **handles** that can be used to reshape and re-size the drawing. Once drawn, objects can have various effects applied to them.

Activity:

1. Start a new blank presentation with a **Title Slide**. Enter the title **Example**, and subtitle **Drawing**.

2. If the **Drawing** toolbar (usually along the lower edge of the display) is not already displayed, select **View | Toolbars** and then select **Drawing**.

3. To change the background colour of the **Title** text box click anywhere in the title, click on the drop down arrow of the **Fill Color** button, , and then select one of the available colours. It is immediately applied to the text box.

4. Click anywhere in the **Subtitle** text box, click on the drop down arrow on the **Fill Color** button and choose a different colour.

5. Click , then click and drag a small box at the bottom right of the slide. Type your name into the text box and apply any fill colour.

6. To delete the box, click on its border and then press <**Delete**>.

7. Leave the presentation open.

Exercise 16 - Object Backgrounds

The range of background options available to slides can also be applied to text boxes and drawn objects.

Activity:

1. Select the **Title** text box used in the previous exercise. To apply an effect click the drop down arrow on the **Fill Color** button, , and choose **Fill Effects** from the menu.

2. Under the **Gradient** tab, change the options for **Colors** and **Shading** styles and see the various effects shown in the **Sample** box. Do not click **OK**.

3. Finally, select the **Two colors** option and a **Shading style** of **Horizontal**.

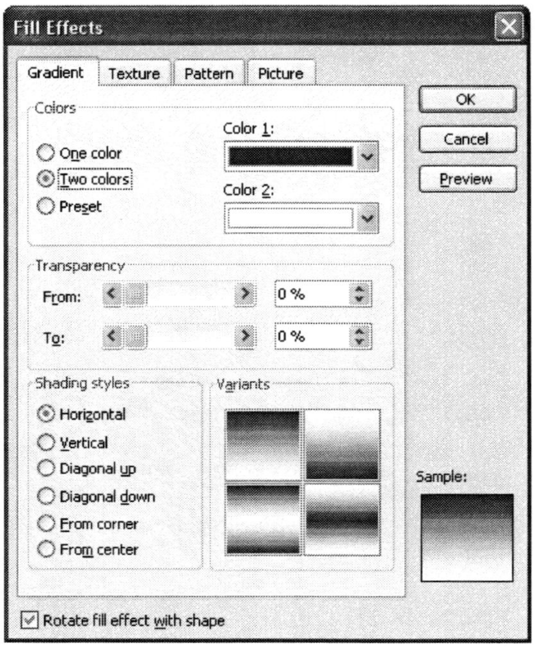

4. Select a dark blue colour for **Color 1** and a lighter blue for **Color 2** and click **OK** to see the effect on the **Title** text box.

5. Click in the **Subtitle** text box, select the **Texture** tab from **Fill Effects** and select the first texture, **Newsprint**. Click **OK** to see the effect on the text box.

6. Click on the **Line** button , and draw a horizontal line between the title text box and subtitle text box.

Note: *A straight line can be drawn by holding down the <**Shift**> key whilst drawing the line.*

7. To change the line style, with the line selected, click the **Line Style** button, , and select **6pt**.

8. To change the line colour, with the line selected, click **Line Style** and select **More Lines**. The **Format AutoShape** dialog box is displayed.

9. Click on the drop down arrow in **Line Color**, from the colour palette, select **Blue**.

10. Click on the drop down arrow in **Line Dashed** and from the drop down list, select the **Square Dot** line style.

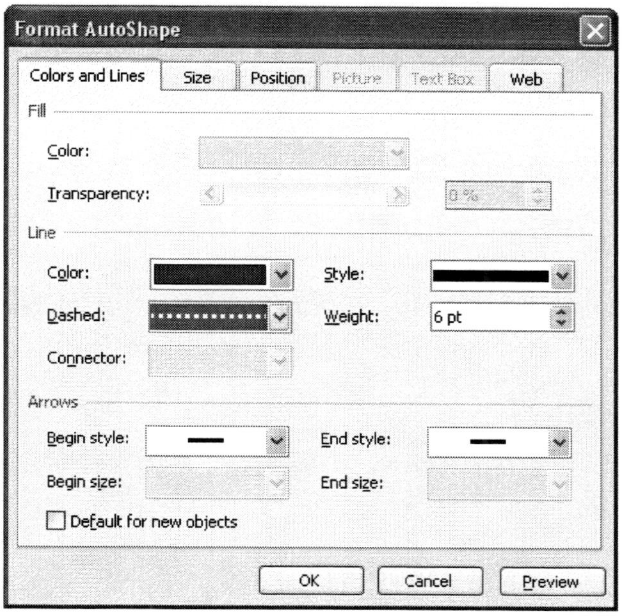

11. Click **OK**.

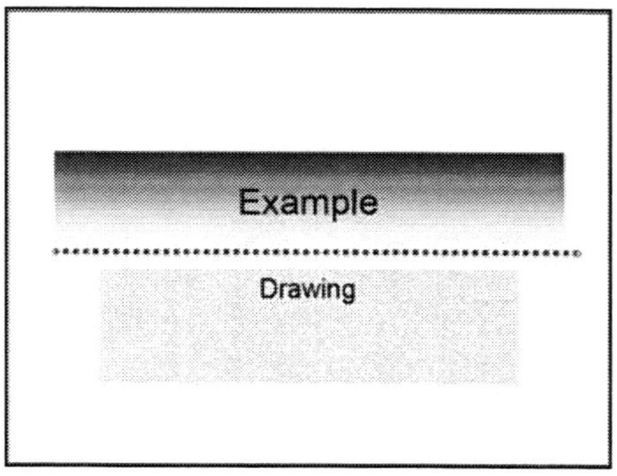

12. Click anywhere in the **Title** text box, click **Line Style** and select **More Lines**.

13. From the **Line Color**, select **Violet**, change the line weight to **3pt**. Click **OK**.

14. Click anywhere in the **Subtitle** text box, click **Line Style** and select **More Lines**, select **Blue-Gray** and **Long Dash Dot**. Click **OK**.

15. Close the presentation <u>without</u> saving.

Exercise 17 - Inserting WordArt

WordArt is a special text feature which can be inserted on to a slide.

Activity:

1. Open the **Holidays** presentation in **Normal View** and ensure that the **Slides** tab is selected at the left.

2. Move to slide **5**, and insert a new **Blank** slide.

3. Click the **Insert WordArt** button, , on the **Drawing** toolbar, to display the **WordArt Gallery**.

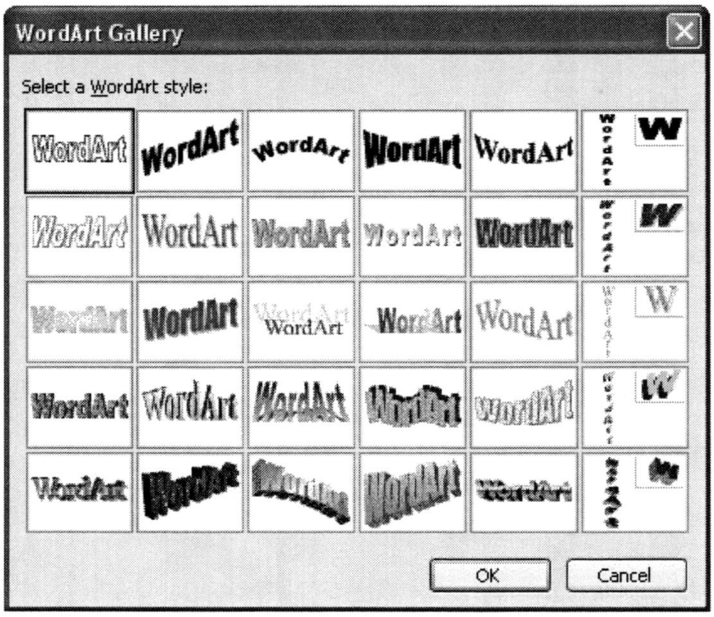

4. Select the first **WordArt** style on the third row, , and click **OK**.

5. In the **Edit WordArt Text** dialog box, type **Why Not ...**, change the font size to **80pt** and click **OK**.

6. The **WordArt** is inserted on the slide. Notice a floating **Word Art** toolbar is displayed on the screen, 

. Point to each button on the toolbar to display a **ToolTip** describing each button. The **WordArt** toolbar disappears when the **WordArt** object is not selected.

7. Click on the text (if the handles around the text are not displayed), point to the middle of the text, hold down the left mouse button and drag the text to the top of the slide, in the centre.

8. With the **WordArt** still selected, click on the small yellow diamond shape at the bottom of the text. Drag this diamond to the left, then to the right to view the effect. Change the **WordArt** back to its original appearance.

9. Click the **Insert WordArt** button again, select the same style **WordArt**, click **OK**.

10. In the **Edit WordArt Text** dialog box, type **Scuba Dive** press <**Enter**>, type **on the Great** press <**Enter**>, type **Barrier Reef?**

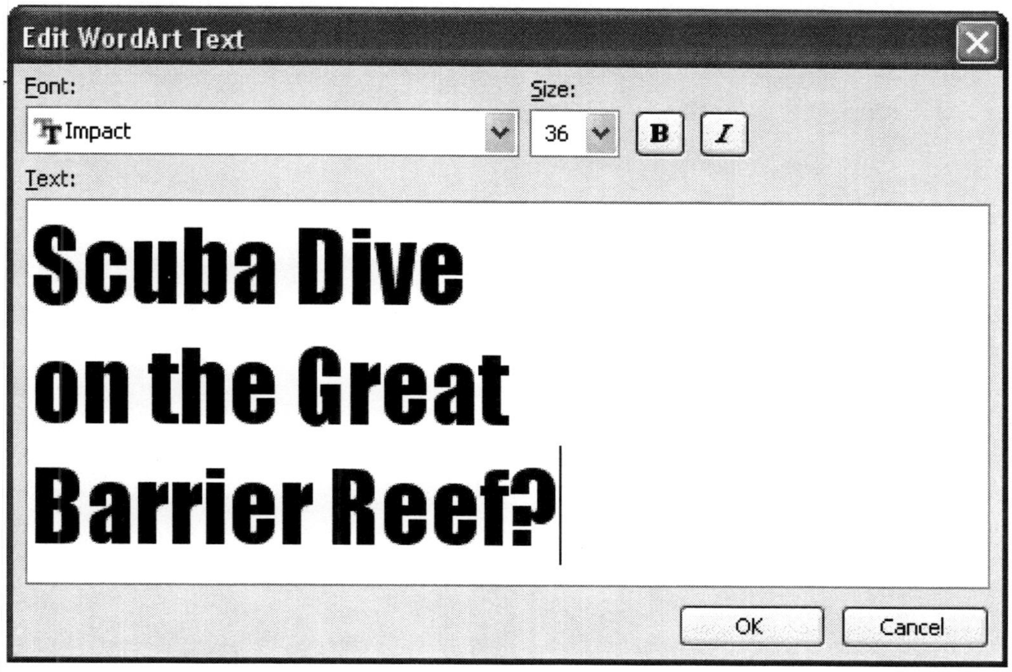

11. Click **OK** and move the text to the left of the slide, just below the title.

12. To alter the character spacing in the text, with the text selected (handles displayed) click on the **WordArt Character Spacing** button, on the **WordArt** toolbar. From the options available, select **Very Loose**. The character spacing is increased.

13. Click the **WordArt Character Spacing** button again, this time select **Tight**.

14. To alter the letter heights, click the **WordArt Same Letter Heights** button, , all the letters are changed to the same height. Click again, the letters are changed back to the original size.

Note: *To edit **WordArt** text, double click on the **WordArt**. To change its style, click the **WordArt Gallery** button, , on the **WordArt** toolbar. Other buttons on the toolbar allow the shape, rotation, etc., of the **WordArt** to be changed.*

15. Save the presentation with the same name and leave it open.

Exercise 18 - Inserting Clip Art

Clip Art is a vast store of pictures, available within all *Microsoft Office* products.

The **Insert Clip Art Task Pane** allows graphics to be found by entering the required descriptive text into the **Search** text box.

> **Note:** *Because of the large number of graphics included with Office 2003, some of them are stored on the CD. If graphics used in the following exercises are unavailable, either insert the 2003 Media Content CD, or replace the specified graphic with an alternative.*

Activity:

1. The **Holidays** presentation should still be open from the previous exercise, if not open it.

2. In **Normal View**, select slide **1**, then select **Insert | Picture | Clip Art**. The **Clip Art Task Pane** appears.

> **Note:** *The **Insert Clip Art** button,* *, from the **Drawing** toolbar can also be used to display the dialog box.*

3. Enter **sun** in the **Search for** text box and click **Go**.

4. Click on the following picture, 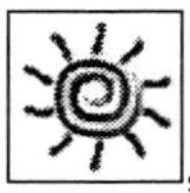, to insert it (or something similar).

5. Move the picture to the **centre** of the slide, below the title and resize appropriately.

6. Save the presentation and leave it open.

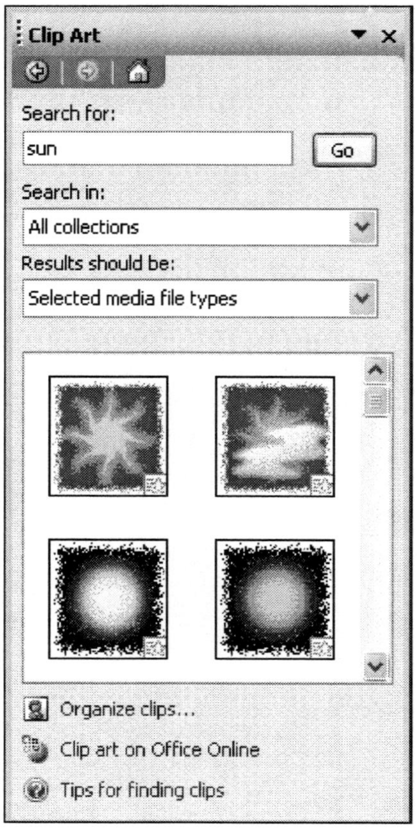

Exercise 19 - Inserting Animated Clips

Animation often helps to get a message across; it can make a presentation dynamic and memorable and help to maintain the interest of your audience. Animated gifs are graphic image files that move, they are usually small in size and don't take up much file space. This type of file is embedded in the presentation, so you don't need to actually save the file separately like you do with movie and sound clips.

A range of animated clips are available from the **Insert Clip Art Task Pane**, normally in **.gif** format. After being inserted into a slide, the animation can be seen when the slide show is previewed. Animated gif pictures also play if the presentation is published as a web page. A symbol beneath a clip in the **Task Pane** indicates it is a motion clip.

Activity:

1. The **Holidays** presentation should still be open from the previous exercise, if not open it.

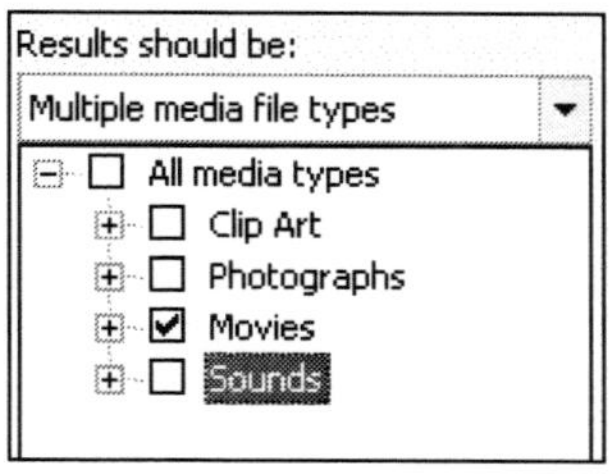

2. In **Normal View**, select slide **3**, **Ski in the Alps**. In the **Clip Art Task Pane** click the **Results should be** drop down list remove all checks except **Movies**.

3. Change the search text to **ski** and click **Go**. Select the following motion clip,  (if this motion clip is not available choose a suitable alternative) and insert it.

Note: *Select an alternative category if no motion clips are available.*

4. Move the picture to the right of the text, below the title and then resize the picture, without obscuring any of the text.

Note: *You cannot change animated gif pictures using the **Picture** toolbar. The changes have to be made in an animated gif editing program before inserting into the slide.*

5. View the slide show for this slide. The **Animated Clip** slide comes into view, the animation can be seen.

6. Press <**Esc**> to end the slide show.

7. Save the presentation and leave it open.

Exercise 20 - Inserting a Picture from a File

Pictures from existing files can be inserted into a slide. This means that many more graphics can be used in a presentation than are available from the **Clip Gallery**. Various image formats are supported, such as **.gif**, **.jpg**, **.tif**, **.png** and **.bmp** (although bitmap files are large).

Activity:

1. The **Holidays** presentation should still be open from the previous exercise, if not open it.

2. Select slide **6** and then select **Insert | Picture | From File**.

3. Select the file **Underwater**, from the data files.

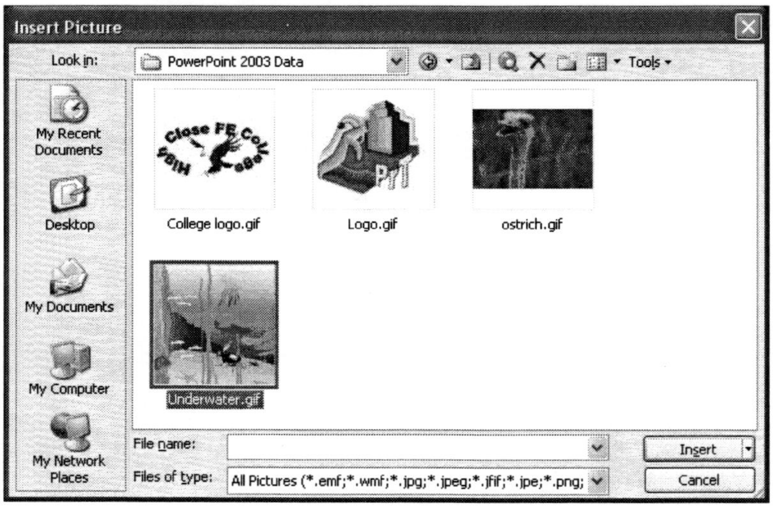

4. Click **Insert**.

5. With the picture selected, move it to the right of the text, below the title as shown below:

6. Save the presentation and close it.

> ***Note:*** *Graphics can be inserted on to the* ***Slide Master****,* ***Title Master*** *and* ***Notes*** *and* ***Handout Masters****.*

7. Open the template **Example** saved in **Exercise 10**. Remember it is in the **Templates** folder, with a path similar to this:

   C:\Documents and Settings\Brian\Application Data\Microsoft\Templates.

8. View the **Slide Master,** if not already displayed.

9. Select **Insert | Picture | From File**.

10. Click on the file **Logo**, then click **Insert**.

11. Move the picture to the top right hand corner of the slide and resize it to less than half the original size. **Right click** on the picture, select **Copy** from the shortcut menu.

12. Switch to the **Title Master** and paste the picture in the same position as on the **Slide Master**.

13. Close **Master View**.

14. Save as a new template with the file name **Company Design**.

15. Close the template.

Exercise 21 - Develop Your Skills

In this exercise the template created in Skill Set 1 will be modified to create a second template.

1. Select **File | Open**, select the **Exercise1** template. This was created earlier in **Exercise 14**.

2. View the **Slide Master** and insert the picture file called **College logo**.

3. Move the picture to the top right corner of the slide.

4. Insert a suitable **Clip Art** image, e.g.  on the **Slide Master** (search for **graduation** and ensure **All media file types** is selected from **Results should be** in the **Task Pane**). Resize and move the image to the bottom left corner of the slide.

5. Create a screen print of the new **Slide Master** and paste it into the **Revision Evidence** document. This is now evidence of a slide master slide and 2 included images. Annotate the picture accordingly.

6. View the **Title Master**, select a suitable animated image from those available in the **Clip Art** gallery and insert it into the top left corner of the slide.

7. Place a copy in the top right corner of the **Title Master**.

8. Select the **Master title style** text box. Using the **Fill Color** button, select one of the lighter scheme colours shown (these appear below **Automatic**).

9. To apply a border, use the **Line Style** button and then **More Lines**. From the **Colors and Lines** tab, select **3pt double line** style, the colour **blue**, **Dash** style.

10. Draw a small rectangular box in the lower right corner of the **Title Master** slide. Apply a gradient fill effect using a pale blue for **Color 1** and white for **Color 2**.

11. Draw a **3pt dark blue** line across the slide, above the footer area, but not touching any images.

12. Create a screen print of the new **Title Master** and paste it into the **Revision Evidence** document replacing the original. This is now evidence of a title master slide, 2 included animated GIFs and included lines, boxes or shading. Annotate the picture accordingly.

13. Return to the **PowerPoint** presentation.

14. Select **File | Page Setup**, set the width to **24cm**, height to **18cm,** slide orientation to **Landscape** and notes orientation to **Portrait**. Create a screen print of the **Page Setup** dialog box with these settings and include it in **Revision Evidence** document. This is evidence of setting page properties.

15. Click **OK** to close **Page Setup**.

16. Save the presentation as a new **Design Template** with the file name **Template1**.

17. Create a screen print of the *PowerPoint* window showing the title bar (**Template1.pot**). Create a screen print of the **Task Pane** showing **Template1** as a template, and paste both images into the *Word* document. This is evidence of the second template. Enter suitable captions below the images.

18. Save the **Revision Evidence** *Word* document and close it.

19. Close all open presentations.

Summary: Images and Drawn Objects

Your ITQ evidence must demonstrate the following skills:

- Format technically complex and interactive presentations using appropriate tools and techniques

You need to know and understand

- How to produce technically complex and interactive presentations. Technically complex and interactive presentations need to be produced using time-line based tools and may include sound and moving images.

Read through the exercises in this Skill Set to give you some ideas of how you could demonstrate these skills.

Skill Set 3

Charts, Tables, Importing & Linking

By the end of this Skill Set you should be able to:

Insert and Format an Organisation Chart
Insert and Import a Table
Insert and Format a Chart
Import a Chart
Link Charts and Text
Modify Linked Data

Exercise 22 - Organisation Charts

Slides in a presentation are composed of various objects which, although easy to insert, can result in an impressive show. When creating a company presentation, it can be a good idea to insert an organisation chart to demonstrate the company's structure. A slide containing a chart can easily be created.

> ***Note:** A prompt for the Office 2003 CD may appear during this exercise.*

Activity:

1. Open the **Progressive Training** presentation.

2. In **Normal View**, move to slide **2**, **Presentation Agenda**.

3. Insert a new slide and from the **Slide Layout Task Pane**, select the **Title and Diagram or Organization Chart** layout, 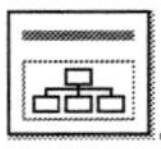.

4. Click to add the title **The Company**.

5. Double click at the point indicated to add the organisation chart and select **Organization Chart** from the **Gallery**.

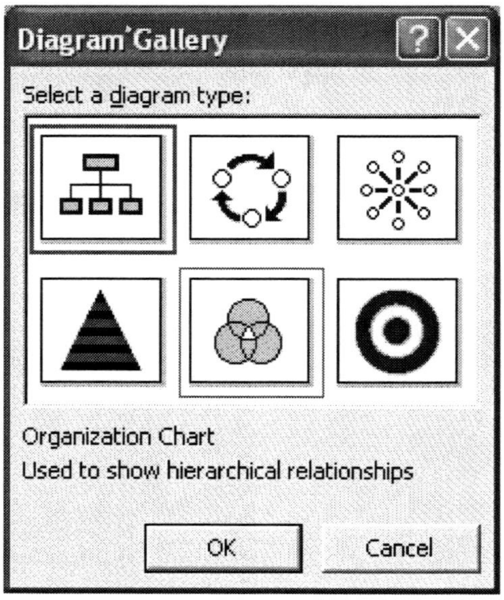

6. Click **OK**. An **Organization Chart** toolbar is displayed when the chart is active. Close the **Task Pane** and zoom in if necessary. Click in the first line of the top box, where it says **Click to add text**.

7. Type **Peter Cooke**, press <**Enter**> and type **Chairman**.

8. Click on the left box on the second level and enter **Barry Evans** on the first line and **Director** on the second line.

9. Click on the right box, second level and enter **Mary Jones** on the first line and **Director** on the second line.

10. The centre box is not needed. Slowly, click on it twice (don't double click) and press <**Delete**>.

11. Two people work for **Barry Evans**: **Joanne Malone**, **Training Manager** and **Katharine Deacon**, **NVQ Supervisor**. Click on Barry Evans' box then from the **Organization Chart** toolbar, click the **Insert Shape** drop down arrow, 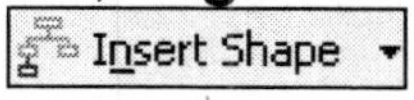

and select **Subordinate**. Repeat this procedure to create the second box. Fill in the above details in the appropriate boxes.

12. Mary Jones, the other Director, has two members of staff who work for her: **Jason Barker**, **Office Manager** and **Maureen Deacon**, **Sales & Marketing**. Create two new subordinate boxes for her. Fill in the above details in the appropriate boxes.

13. Notice how the boxes are automatically rescaled.

14. Jason Barker has a co-worker. Select his box and from the **Insert Shape** drop down list, select **Coworker** and add **Janet Johnson**, **Accounts**.

15. Continue adding to the organisation chart until it resembles the example shown below. The layout shown is the default, but could be created by selecting the box for **Joanne Malone**, clicking **Layout** on the **Organization Chart** toolbar and choosing **Right Hanging**. Repeat for **Janet Johnson**.

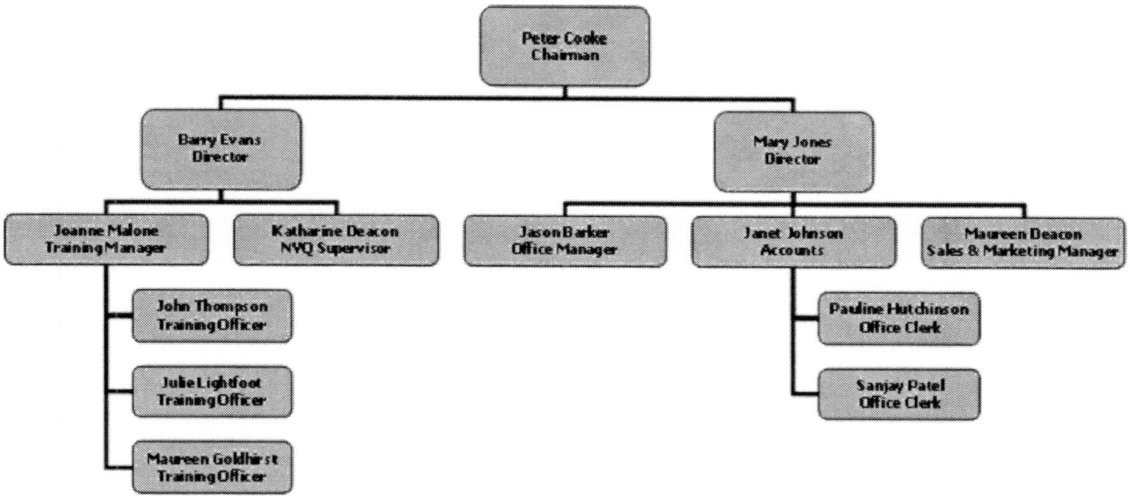

16. Click away from the chart to anchor it on the slide.

17. Save the presentation with the same name and leave it open.

Exercise 23 - Formatting Organisation Charts

Organisation charts can be formatted to change colours, fonts, etc.

Activity:

1. The **Progressive Training** presentation should be open from the previous exercise, if not open it.

2. Make sure you are viewing the organisation chart in **Normal View**.

3. Click on the chart to select it.

4. To change the colour of the text, click the **Font Color** drop down arrow and choose **blue** from the options.

5. To change the font, select **Format | Font** and from the **Font** dialog box, select the **Times New Roman**, **Bold** font style.

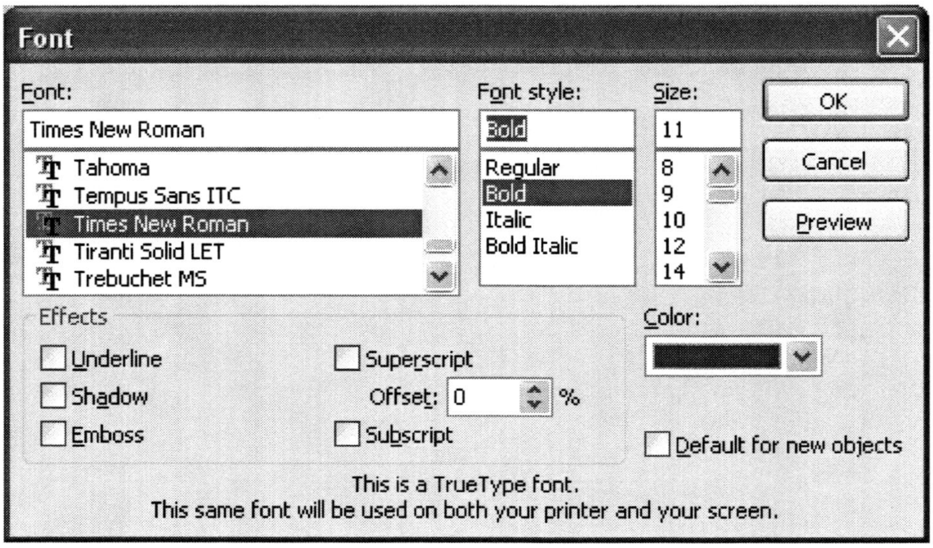

6. Click **OK**.

7. To change the colour of the boxes click **Autoformat**,  from the **Organization Chart** toolbar.

8. Select **3-D Color** from the **Gallery**.

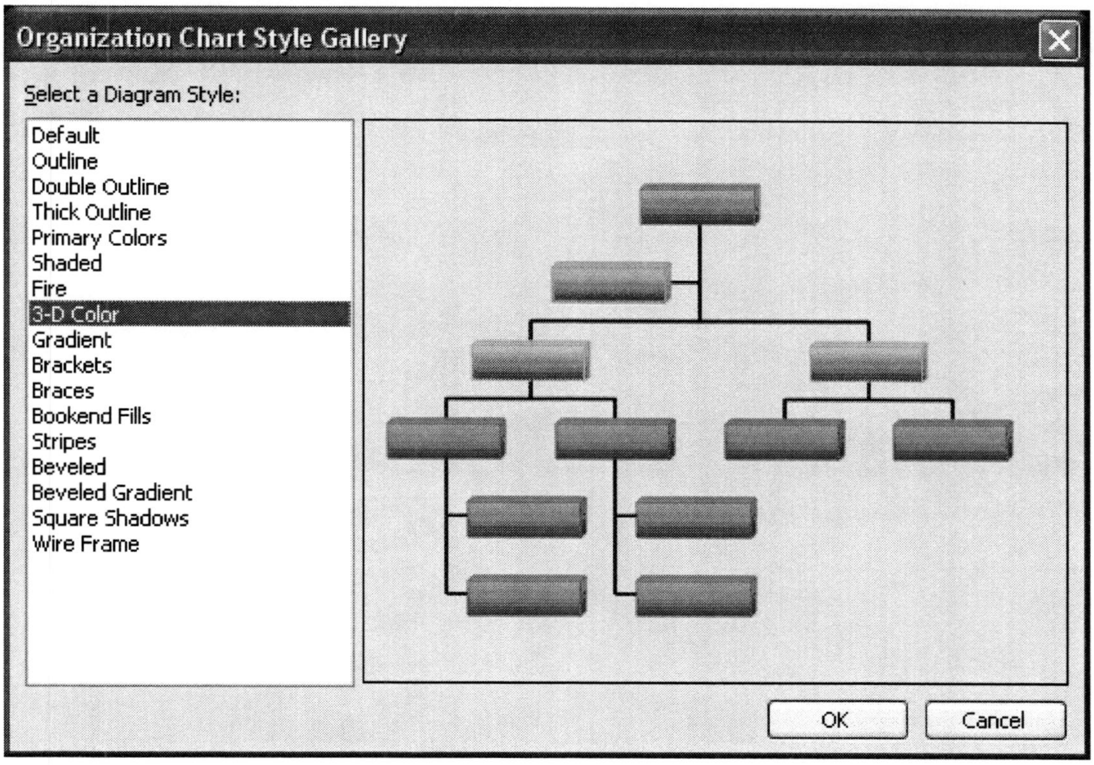

9. Click **OK**.

> ***Note:*** *Borders can be applied from the* ***Organization Chart Style Gallery*** *by choosing one of the* ***Outline*** *styles.*

10. Select **Format | Slide Design**.

11. Scroll down the **Task Pane** and select **Company Design** (you may need to use the **Browse** link at the bottom of the pane). All the features of this layout are applied to all slides in the presentation.

12. Save the presentation and leave it open.

Exercise 24 - Inserting a Table

Tables can be a useful tool for aligning data in multiple column lists. Tables can be created within *PowerPoint*, or they can be imported from another application such as *Excel*.

Activity:

1. The **Progressive Training** presentation should be open from the previous exercise, if not open it.
2. View slide **5**, **The Products**, in **Normal View**.
3. Insert a new slide, based on the **Title and Table** layout.

> **Note:** *Alternatively, select **Insert | Table**.*

4. Double click on the icon.
5. From the dialog box, select **2** columns by **7** rows and then click **OK**. A table appears on the slide and the **Tables and Borders** toolbar is displayed.
6. Enter the slide title **Product Costs**.
7. Enter the data below into the table, using the <**Tab**> key to move from cell to cell.

Product	Price £
Open Learning Guides	20
Trainers Packs	100
New CLAIT Per Unit	15
CLAIT Plus Per Unit	15
CLAIT Advanced Per Unit	30
ECDL Per Module	15

8. Change the size of all text in the table to **24pt** - you will only need to select the table rather than the text (click on the table border).
9. With the table selected, click the **Fill Color**, , drop down arrow and select a pale colour to fill the table.
10. If necessary, click and drag the border between columns to the right so all text is on a single line.

> **Note:** *It is possible to resize any cells by clicking and dragging the margins. Fonts, text and line colour can all be used to format the table, using the usual techniques.*

11. Save the presentation and close it.

12. Start a new, blank presentation with a **Title Only** slide. You are going to import a table from an *Excel* worksheet.

13. Start *Excel* and open the workbook **Product Sales** from the data files. Make sure the **Data** sheet is displayed, as this worksheet contains the table to be imported.

14. Save the workbook and close *Excel*.

15. On the blank slide, add the title **Excel Table** and select **Insert | Object**.

16. Select the **Create from file** option and click **Browse**.

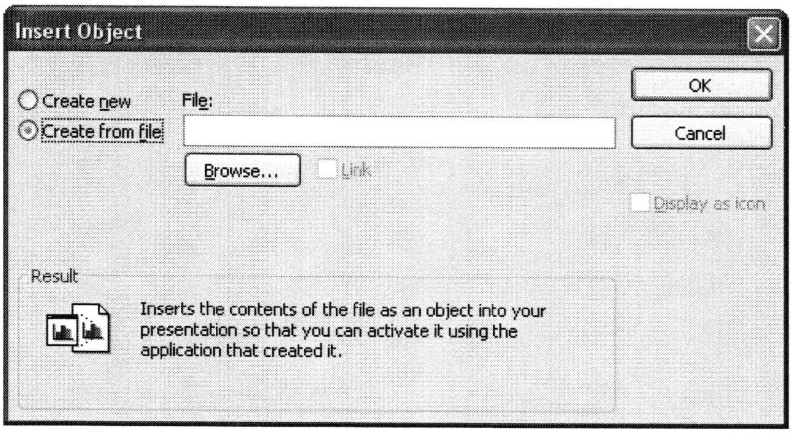

17. Select the file **Product Sales** from the data file location and click **OK**.

> ***Note:*** *To create a link to this spreadsheet so you would be prompted to update the presentation if the source data in Excel changed, you would check the **Link** box. Do not check the box now.*

18. Click **OK** to import the table.

19. Double click on the table to activate *Excel* within the slide. Change the quantity of **New CLAIT** sales for **Feb** to **45**.

20. Select the cell containing the title **Product Sales Jan-Apr** and change its fill colour to pale green. Change the font to **Times New Roman 18pt**.

21. Click on an area away from the table and notice how it has changed.

> ***Note:*** *A table may be imported from Access. To do this, start Access and open the database. From the database window, select the required table and then select **Edit | Copy**. Close Access. On the slide select **Edit | Paste**. This is only really suitable if the Access table is small enough to fit on the slide. Like an imported Excel table, you can double click on the table to edit the data or format the table.*

22. Close the presentation without saving.

Exercise 25 - Inserting Charts

A chart can be inserted on to a slide to display data in a more attractive way. The relevant information is entered into a datasheet and is then converted into a chart.

Activity:

1. Start a new blank presentation.

2. From the **Slide Layout Task Pane**, select the **Title and Chart** layout, 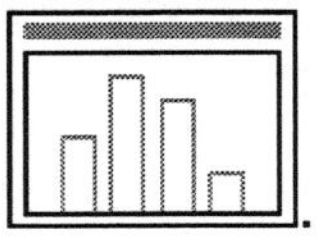.

3. Add the title **Sales Figures**.

4. Double click where indicated to add the chart. By default a **3D Column** chart is created.

5. Amend the **Datasheet** as shown below:

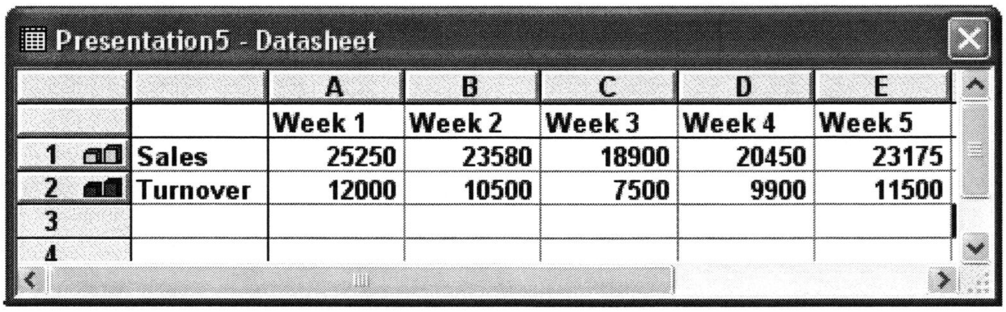

		A	B	C	D	E
		Week 1	Week 2	Week 3	Week 4	Week 5
1	Sales	25250	23580	18900	20450	23175
2	Turnover	12000	10500	7500	9900	11500
3						
4						

> ***Note:*** *To clear the contents from row 3 and so clear the legend entry, right click on the row 3 heading in the datasheet and select* ***Clear Contents.***

6. Close the datasheet.

7. Click at the edge of the slide, to anchor the chart on to the slide.

8. To change the chart type, double click on the chart to edit it and select **Chart | Chart Type**. From the **Standard Types** tab, select **Line,** from the **Chart sub-type,** select **Line with markers displayed at each data value**. Click **OK**.

9. Click at the edge of the slide to view the changes.

10. Save the presentation as **Charts** and leave it open.

Exercise 26 - Formatting Charts

Fonts and colours of all parts of a chart can be changed.

Activity:

1. Open the **Charts** presentation, if not open already from the previous exercise.

2. Double click on the chart to edit it.

***Note:** Use **ToolTips** to identify areas of the chart for editing, if required.*

3. Double clicking on any part of the chart displays the formatting dialog box for that area. Double click on the **Plot Area** (not on a gridline) to display the **Format Plot Area** dialog box.

4. Click **Fill Effects** from the **Area** section. Make sure the **Gradient** tab is selected. Select **Two colors**. From the **Color 1** drop down list, select **Blue** and from **Color 2**, select **Light Turquoise**.

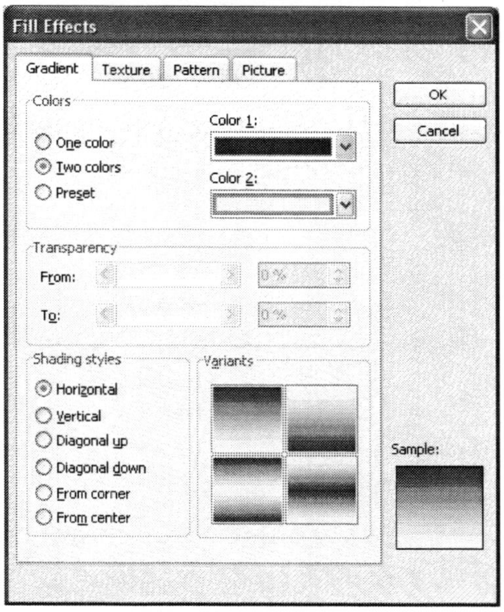

5. Click **OK** to apply the colours and click **OK** again to return to the chart.

***Note:** An alternative method of editing is to right click on the object, then select **Format...** from the shortcut menu.*

6. Change the **Chart Area** colour to **light blue**, then click **OK**.

7. Double click on the horizontal **Category Axis** (x-axis) to display the **Format Axis** dialog box.

8. Select the **Font** tab and change the font to **Tempus Sans ITC** (or another font if this is unavailable) and click **OK**.

9. Double click on the legend at the right of the chart and select the **Font** tab.

10. Change the font to **Tempus Sans ITC** and click **OK**.

11. To change the line colour and line style, double click on the **Turnover series**, the **Format Data Series** dialog box is displayed.

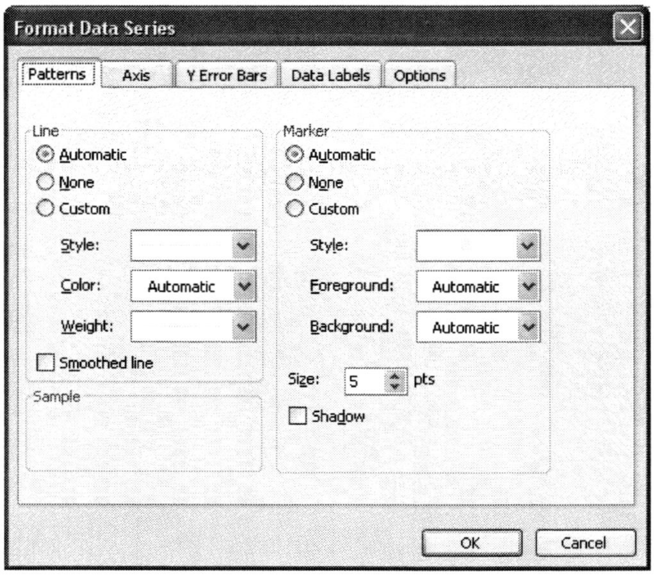

12. With the **Patterns** tab selected, click on the **Line Style** drop down list, select a broken line.

13. In the **Line** section from the **Color** drop down list, select the colour **blue,** change the line weight to the third option.

14. In the **Marker** section click on the **Style** drop down arrow, select the **triangle** style. Choose a different foreground and background colour. Click **OK**.

15. Double click on the **Sales series** and format the series using a different line style, marker style and colour.

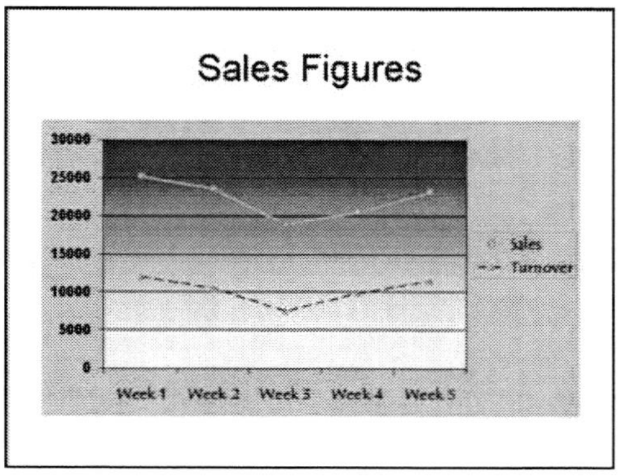

16. Save the presentation and close it.

Exercise 27 - Importing a Chart

Data can be imported into *PowerPoint* from spreadsheets, rather than create a chart from scratch, if a suitable one already exists within a workbook.

Activity:

1. Open the presentation **Progressive Training**.

2. Insert a new **Title Only** slide at the end of the presentation. Insert the title **Product Sales**.

3. Start *Excel* and open the workbook **Product Sales** from the data files.

4. With the **Sales Jan - Apr** sheet tab displayed, select the chart and click **Copy**, .

5. Switch to *PowerPoint* and with the **Product Sales** slide selected, select **Edit | Paste Special** and select **Paste**, if not already selected. Do not check **Display as icon**.

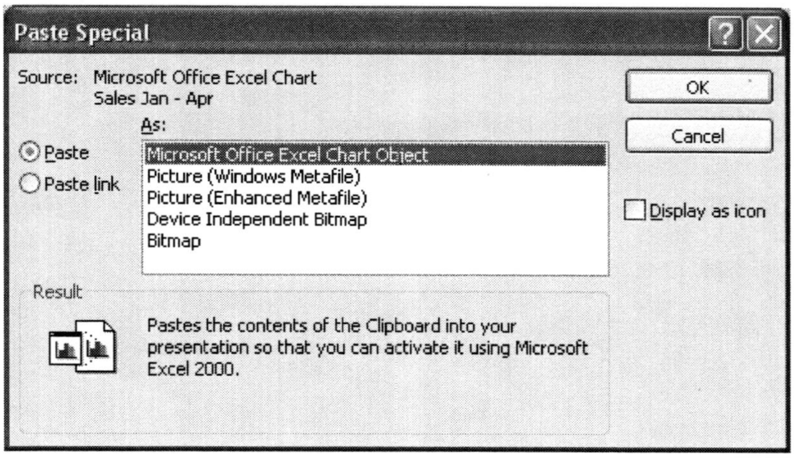

6. Click **OK** to paste the chart on to the slide. Resize as appropriate. Save the presentation and leave it open.

7. You should produce evidence of the imported chart in its original application. Switch to *Excel*, with the **Sales Jan - Apr** sheet tab selected create a screen print of the chart.

8. Open the **Evidence** document and paste in the screen print. Enter a suitable caption under the image.

9. From *PowerPoint* take a screen print of the chart slide and paste it into the **Evidence** document. Enter a caption explaining that this is the pasted chart.

10. Save and close the document. Close *Word*. Close *Excel*.

11. Close the presentation, saving any changes if prompted.

Exercise 28 - Linking

Objects on a slide can be linked to external data from a variety of other applications. Linking an object means that if its source data is changed, those changes can be reflected in the object. It also means that the source data can be opened directly from *PowerPoint*.

Activity:

1. Open the presentation **Retreat**, create a new **Title Only** slide after slide **7 Price List**, which will contain a linked chart. Add the title **Occupancy**.

2. Start *Excel* and open the workbook **Occupancy** from the data files.

3. With the **Occupancy levels** sheet tab displayed, select the chart and click **Copy**, .

4. Use the **Taskbar** to return to *PowerPoint*.

5. With the **Occupancy** slide selected, select **Edit | Paste Special** and select **Paste link**. Do not check **Display as icon**.

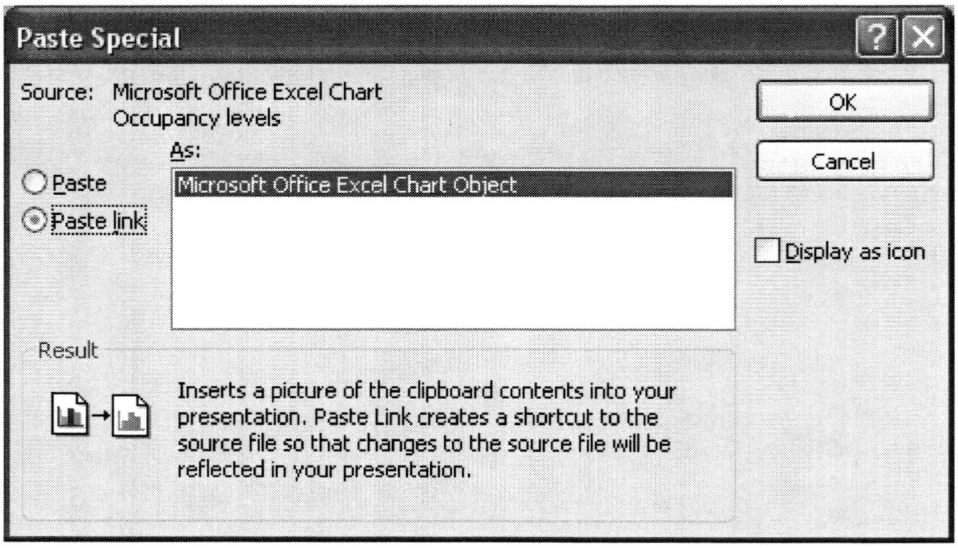

6. Click **OK** to paste the linked chart on to the slide.

7. Save the presentation as **Links** and leave it open.

8. Close the *Excel* spreadsheet.

9. Create another new **Title Only** slide after slide **8 Occupancy**. This will contain a linked text file. Add the title **Testimonials**.

10. To create the link, select **Insert | Object** and the **Create from file** option.

11. Click **Browse** and locate the data files. Select the **Comments** file.

12. Click **OK** and in the **Insert Object** dialog box, check **Link**.

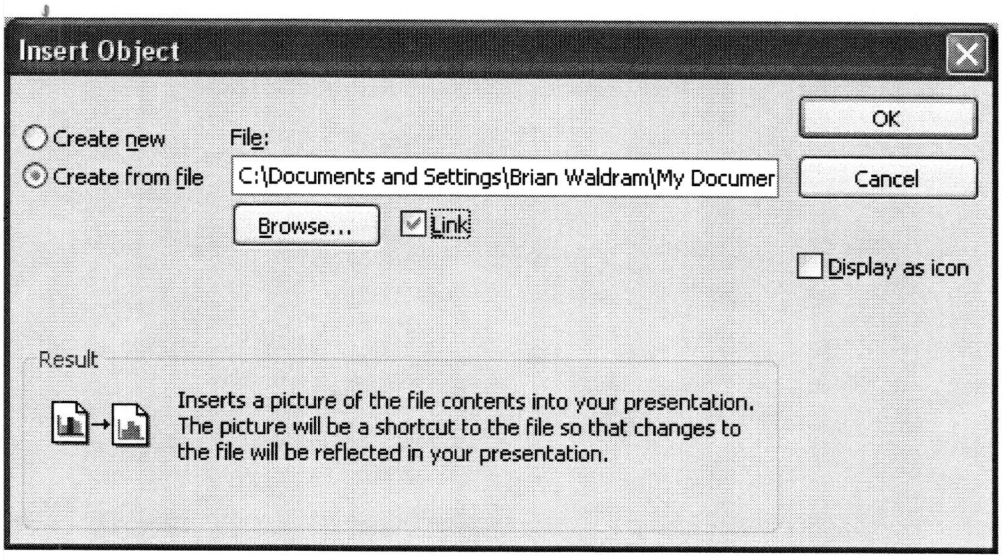

13. Click **OK** to insert the linked object.

14. Save the presentation.

15. To view the document, double click the object. *Word* starts and opens the source document.

16. Close *Word*.

17. Save the presentation and close it.

Exercise 29 - Modifying Linked Data

Whenever a presentation containing links is opened, you will always be prompted to update the links. If the option is accepted, all linked objects within the presentation will be updated with the current versions from the source data. If not, they will be left unchanged.

Activity:

1. Open the *Excel* spreadsheet **Occupancy**.

2. Select the worksheet **Occupancy levels**.

3. Double click on any column.

4. To change the colour of the data series, with the **Patterns** tab of the **Format Data Series** dialog box selected, choose green from the **Area** colour grid.

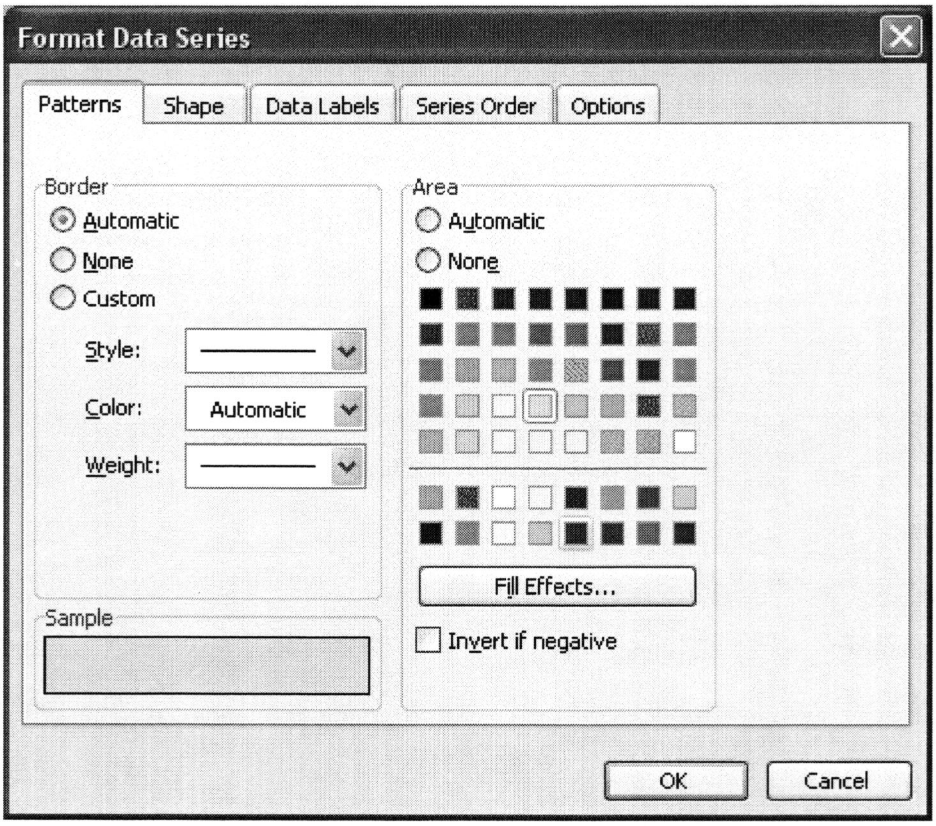

5. Click **OK**.

6. Save the spreadsheet and leave it open.

7. Open *Word* and the document **Comments**. Add the following text after the final comment, ignoring the format for now:

   This retreat has made life feel good again
   Wendy Williams, Birmingham

8. Use the **Format Painter** to standardise the formatting of the new text.

9. Save the document with the same name and close *Word*.

10. In *PowerPoint* open the presentation **Links** - the following prompt appears:

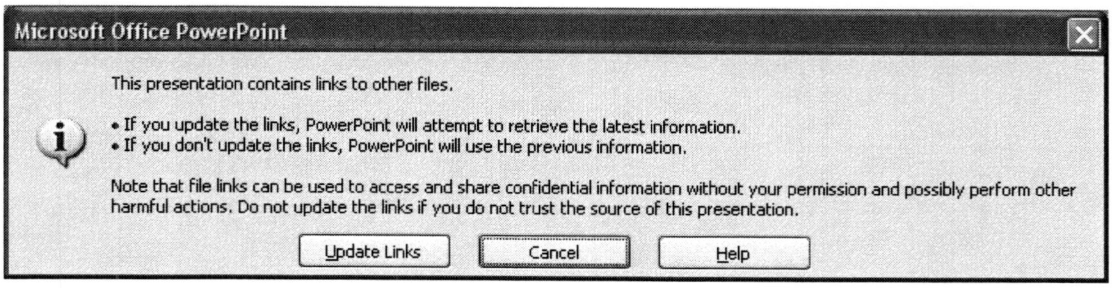

11. Click **Update Links**.

12. View slide **9** to see that the text added in *Word* has also been changed in *PowerPoint*.

13. View slide **8** (linked chart) to see that the data series changed to green in *Excel* has also been changed in *PowerPoint*.

14. Save the presentation and close it.

15. Close *Excel*.

Exercise 30 - Develop Your Skills

1. Open the **High Close** presentation. This presentation has been supplied on disk to save you time. For your evidence, you will be expected to create all presentations yourself.

2. You have decided to use **Template1** created in **Exercise 21** for your design. Apply the design template **Template1**.

3. Move to slide **8**, **How Will We Get There?**

4. Insert a new **Organization Chart** slide.

5. Insert the slide title **New Organisation** and create the organisation chart as shown below. The layout of the lower boxes is **Right Hanging**.

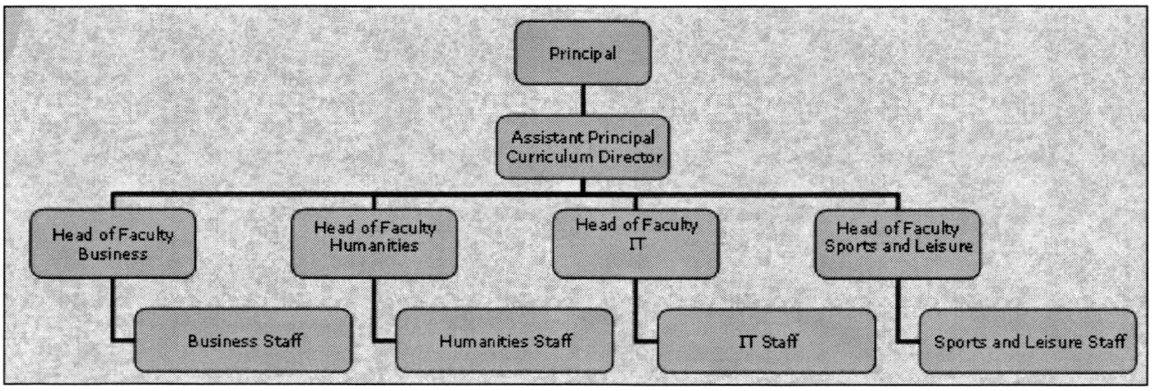

6. Change the font to **Copperplate Gothic Bold**, colour **dark blue**, size **10pt**.

7. **Autoformat** the boxes with the **Square Shadows** style.

8. Ensure the organisation chart fills the slide, resizing if necessary (use the **Fit Text** button on the **Organization Chart** toolbar if text appears outside the boxes).

9. Move to slide **10**, **Market Research**.

10. Insert a new **Title and Chart** slide.

11. Insert the title **Gender Split** and amend the datasheet as shown below:

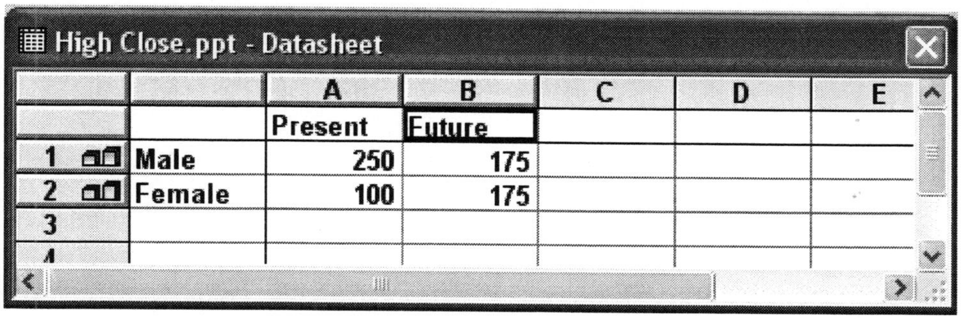

12. Apply a gradient effect to the **Male** data series and a different effect to the **Female** data series.

13. Change the **Category Axis** font to **Italics**.

14. Insert a new **Title and Table** slide, after slide **7**.

15. Enter the slide title **Funding**. Enter the data below into the table.

Organisation	Percentage
LSC	30%
Government	40%
Awarding Bodies	15%
Franchise Agreements	10%
Local Councils	5%

16. Change the font size to **30pt** (you will have to type the figure into the **Font Size** box), the font to **Baskerville Old Face** (or an alternative if this is unavailable). **Centre** align all text in the **Percentage** column.

17. Insert a new **Title Only** slide, after slide **5** and enter the title **Retention Rates**.

18. Start *Excel* and open the workbook **Retention Rate**.

19. With the **Retention Rate** sheet tab selected, copy the chart.

20. In *PowerPoint*, select **Edit | Paste** to paste the chart on to the slide.

21. Move to slide **3 Where Are We Now?**. Insert this animated clip, , using the search **Emotions** (if this animated clip is not available choose a suitable alternative, from another category if necessary).

22. Increase the size of the image.

23. Move to slide **15**, **Threats** and insert this animated clip, , using the same search results.

24. Move the image to the bottom right of the slide. Enlarge the image ensuring that it does not obscure any text.

25. View the slide show to view the animated clips.

26. Save the presentation.

27. Create a screen print of the imported chart, **Retention Rate**, in *Excel*.

28. Paste it into the **Revision Evidence** document. Enter a suitable caption below the image.

29. Save the document and close it.

30. Close *Excel*.

31. Close the presentation.

Summary - Charts, Tables, Importing & Linking

Your ITQ evidence must demonstrate the following skills:

- Export and import, link objects between different software
- Make references to external data. For example: hyperlinks, object linking and embedding.

Read through the exercises in this Skill Set to give you some ideas of how you could demonstrate these skills.

Skill Set 4

Multimedia

By the end of this Skill Set you should be able to:

Insert Sound from Files

Insert Movie Clips

Edit a Video Clip

Use Preset and Custom Animation

Animate a Chart

Exercise 31 - Inserting Sounds

Sounds can be used in presentations in various ways. A sound can be added to a slide or to an animation effect (see **Exercise 34**), so that it plays when the slide is viewed, or when the animation is activated. This type of sound is known as a **sound event** and can be played on mouse click, for a single slide, or set to play for several slides using **Effect Options**.

Alternatively, sounds can be set up to play as a background throughout a presentation - this is sometimes called **streaming sound**. You could use an audio track from CD to do this, although you would always need to have the CD in the CD drive in order to play it. A voice narration can be recorded to play in a presentation, perhaps if the show was to run on its own without a presenter, for example. Narration takes precedence over other sounds on a slide. You will need a microphone to record and digitise a voice recording. If you need to edit or cut the sound clip, separate editing software will be required.

Sounds are linked to a presentation by default, to save space. This means that for the sound to play it must be stored with the presentation. If the show is presented on a different computer, the sound file must also be installed on that computer. However, it is possible to embed a sound file so that it becomes part of the presentation, but this makes the file size much larger. Various formats are supported, e.g. **MIDI**, **MP3**, **.wav** and **.wma** files.

Activity:

1. Open the **Holidays** presentation and move to slide **2**.
2. To insert a sound select **Insert | Movies and Sounds | Sound from File** (to insert a CD track you would select **Play Audio CD Track**).
3. From **Look in** select **Local Disk C:\Windows\Media** and select any sound file.
4. Click **OK** and the following prompt appears.

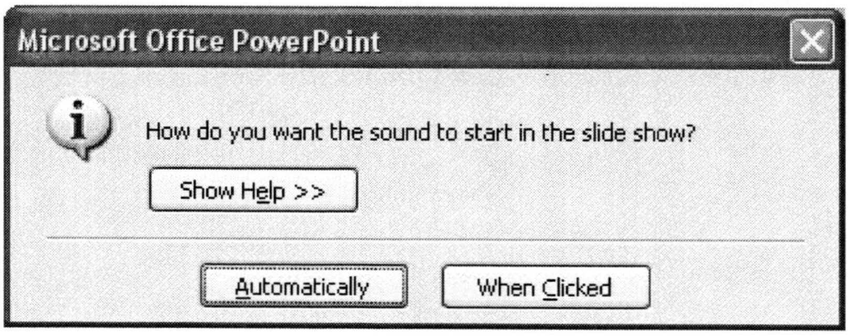

5. Click **Automatically** for the sound to start without any manual intervention.

6. Click the **Slide Show** button. The sound will play when the slide appears. Press <**Esc**>.

7. To control when the sound will play, select **Slide Show | Custom Animation** and the **Custom Animation Task Pane** appears.

8. The entry in the **Task Pane** represents the sound, with a corresponding number on the slide. Click the drop down list at the right of the item and select **Timing**.

9. To change the timing, set the time to start **After Previous** event with a **Delay** of **5 seconds**.

10. Click **OK** then click the **Slide Show** button. The slide will appear and 5 seconds later the sound will play. Press <**Esc**>.

11. To create a 'previous event' to trigger the sound, select the graphic of the small boy and the sandcastle.

12. To add an effect, click Add Effect from the **Custom Animation** task pane and select **Entrance** then **Zoom** (you may need to select **More effects** first, then click **OK**).

13. **Picture frame 4** appears in the **Task Pane**. Click the **Re-Order Up** button, , so that it occurs before the sound. Now the sound will play 5 seconds after the image is animated.

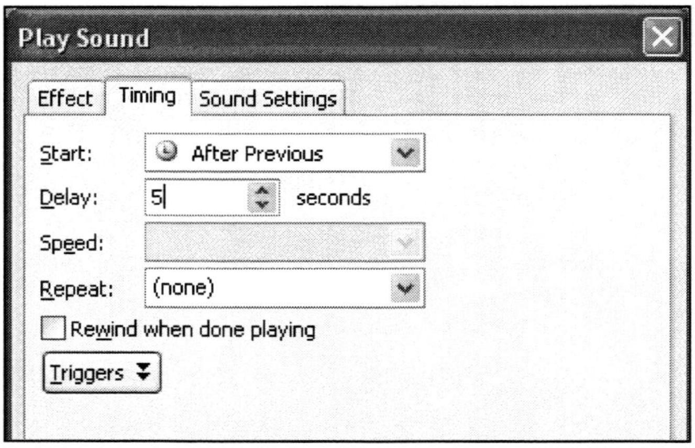

14. With **Picture frame 4** still selected, in the task pane, select **After Previous** from the **Start** drop down list. Click the drop down arrow for the item, select **Timing** and set a time delay of 4 seconds. Click **OK**.

15. Click the **Slide Show** button, . The slide appears without the sandcastle image. After 4 seconds the image 'zooms' in, and after a further 5 seconds the sound will play.

16. Stop the show, save the presentation as **Holidays2** and leave it open.

Exercise 32 - Inserting Movies

Movies are also easily added to slides. Finished movie files that you have on file can be inserted, or if you have video editing software you can actually edit and render (apply effects to) a movie before exporting it to *PowerPoint*. This is technically complex but covered very basically in the next exercise.

Activity:

1. Open the **Holidays2** presentation, if not open already from the previous exercise.
2. Insert a new **Title Only** slide at the end of the presentation.
3. Add the title **Brought to you by:**
4. To insert a video clip select **Insert | Movies and Sounds | Movie from File**.
5. Locate the data folder and select the **cia.avi** file and click **OK**. The following prompt appears:

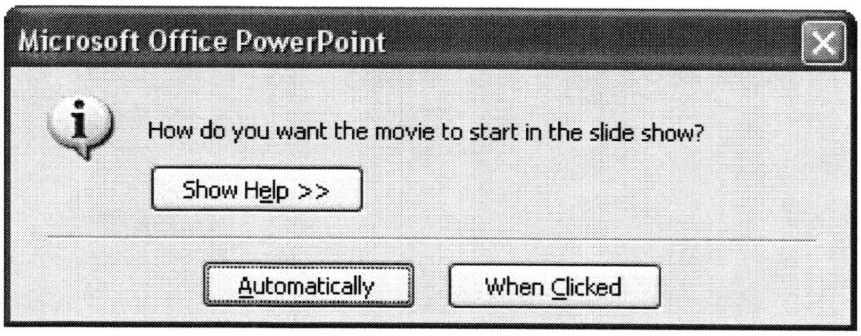

6. Select **Automatically** so that the movie will automatically play.
7. Click the **Slide Show** button to view the current slide in action.
8. When the animation has finished, press <**Esc**> to end the show.
9. To change the movie so that it plays only when the mouse is clicked, select it and then select **Slide Show | Custom Animation**.

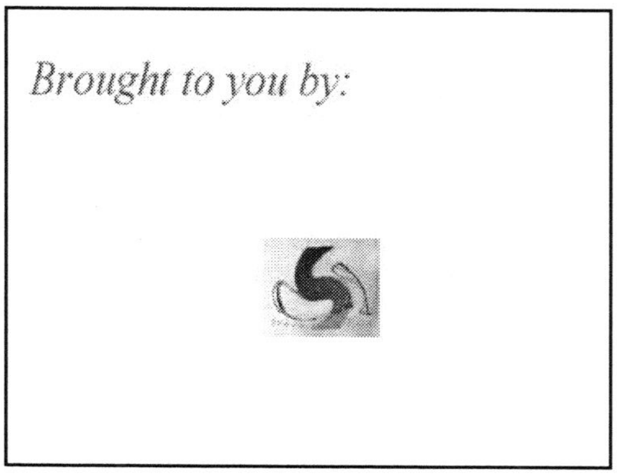

10. Click the drop down arrow for the movie and select **Start on Click**.
11. View the slide show for this slide again.

12. Click to see the movie (the animation will not start until the mouse is clicked), then when the movie finishes press <**Esc**> to end the show.

13. To change the movie so that it plays continuously, right click on the movie on the slide.

14. Select **Edit Movie Object**.

15. Check **Loop until stopped**.

16. Click **OK**.

17. View the slide show for this slide again. Click to start the movie; it will play continuously until you press <**Esc**>. Press <**Esc**>.

18. Press <**Esc**> again to end the show.

19. Save the presentation and leave it open.

***Note:** You should produce evidence showing the video clip object.*

20. Click <u>once</u> on the video **cia**, select **Insert | Movies and Sounds | Movie from File**, to display the **Insert Movie** dialog box. Create a screen print. Click **Cancel** to close the dialog box.

21. Open the **Evidence** document and paste in the screen print.

22. Enter a suitable description beneath the image. Save and close the document. Close *Word.*

23. Save and close the presentation.

Exercise 33 - Video Editing

Video editing can be a complex process and a whole book could be dedicated to this subject. It cannot be done within *PowerPoint* and this exercise demonstrates basic video editing using *Windows Movie Maker*. Further editing techniques are beyond the scope of this guide. Various movie formats can be used by *PowerPoint*, such as **.avi**, **.mov**, **.qt**, **.mpg**, **.mpeg** and **.wmv**.

Activity:

1. Select **Start | All Programs | Accessories | Windows Movie Maker**.

2. Select **File | Import into Collections**. From the data location, select **launch.mpeg** and click **Import**.

3. From the lower area of the screen, click **Show Timeline**, 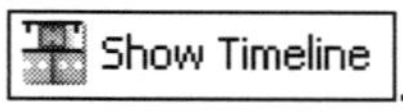

.

4. Drag the **launch** thumbnail to the timeline area.

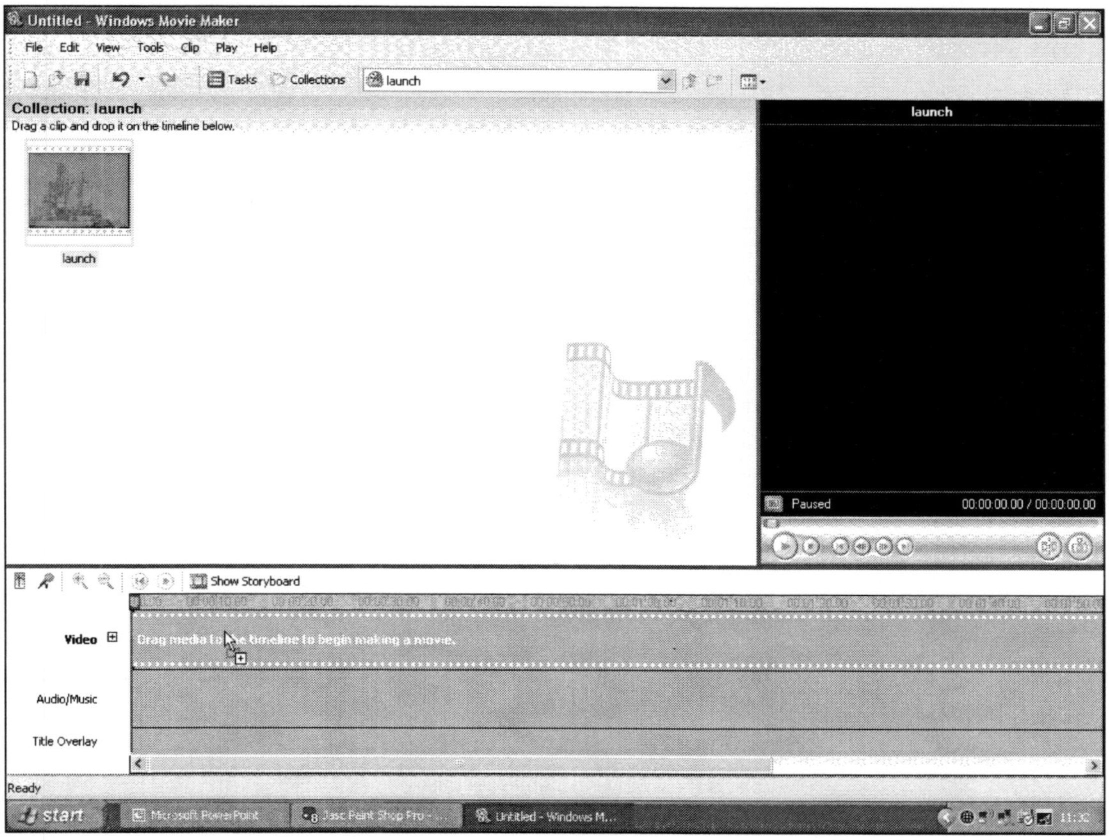

5. Click **Play**, , at the bottom of the viewing panel on the right to see the original movie clip.

6. The clip is to be shortened to about 8 seconds long. Click and drag the right handle in the timeline to the left until it reaches about 8 seconds (shown as a tooltip).

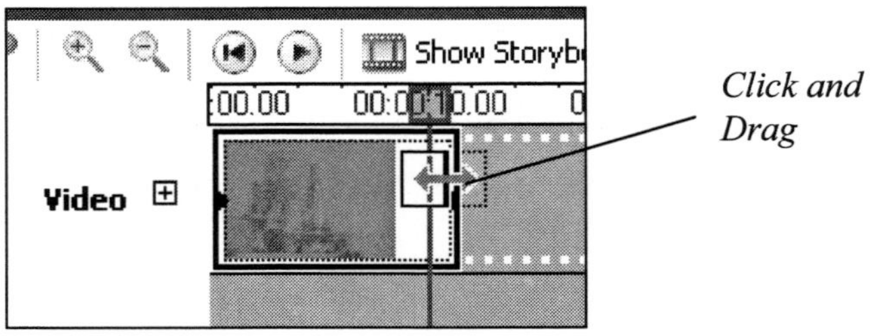

7. Play the clip again - notice how the editing has affected its length.

8. The edited clip can be used in *PowerPoint*. Select **File | Save Movie File** and select **My computer**, then click **Next**.

9. Enter the file name **short launch** and click **Browse** to specify the saving location as the data folder.

10. Click **Next** and then **Next** again. Uncheck **Play Movie...** and click **Finish**.

11. Start a new presentation with a blank slide.

12. To import the edited video clip, select **Insert | Movies and Sounds | Movie from File**.

13. From the **Insert Movie** dialog box, locate the data files and select the file **short launch.wmv**.

14. Click **OK**.

15. Click **Automatically** when prompted and view the slide show.

16. End the show after you've seen the clip.

17. Close the presentation without saving.

18. Close *Windows Movie Maker* without saving any projects.

Exercise 34 - Introducing Animation

It has been seen that different items on a slide can be animated using *PowerPoint*. These items can be introduced with a click of the mouse, or automatically after a specified time.

Activity:

1. Open the **Holidays2** presentation. In **Normal View**, with slide **1** selected, ensure the **Custom Animation Task Pane** is displayed.

2. Select the **WordArt** from the slide and click **Add Effect**.

3. Choose **Entrance | More Effects | Bounce** (from the **Exciting** section) and click **OK**.

4. Click the drop down arrow for the effect and select **Effect Options**.

5. Choose **Drum Roll** from the **Sound** drop down list.

6. Select the **Timing** tab. To start animation manually make sure **On Click** is selected from **Start** and click **OK**.

7. Now select the sun graphic and click **Add Effect**. Add a **Pinwheel** entrance effect and the sound **Breeze**.

8. Click **OK** to apply the effects and ensure **On Click** is selected from **Start**, then save the presentation.

9. View the slide show. Click the mouse button to trigger the text entry animation, then again to introduce the picture. Right click and select **End Show**.

10. Set the animation for both objects to **Start After Previous**, with a **5 second** delay.

11. Click **OK** and view the show again but this time do not click the mouse button. Notice the animation is now activated automatically. End the show.

12. Save the presentation and leave it open.

Exercise 35 - Animation Sequences

The order in which objects are animated can be changed. What happens after they are animated can also be specified; these sequences are known as **builds**. It is important to appreciate that sometimes you may want to have a consistent look to animations, rather than many different effects that may appear slightly over the top. This will help to give a feeling of coherence to the presentation.

Activity:

1. Display slide **1** of the **Holidays2** presentation in **Normal View**.
2. To apply the picture's animation first, from the **Custom Animation** task pane, select the picture entry and click **Re-order Up**, .

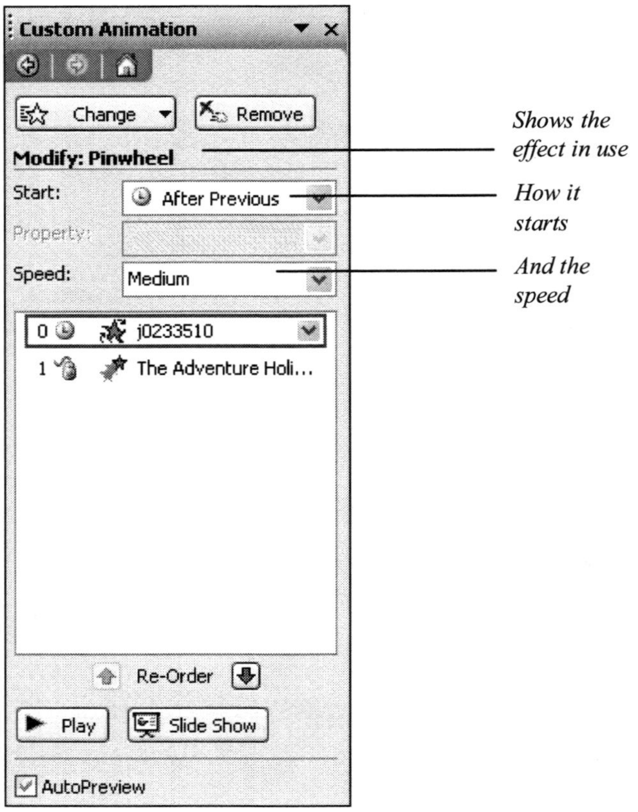

3. View the slide show for the first slide and notice how the picture now appears first. End the show.
4. Change the animation sequence back to how it was originally.
5. Save the changes to the presentation and close it.
6. Open the **Progressive Training** presentation.

7. In **Normal View**, move to slide **2 Presentation Agenda**, viewing the **Custom Animation Task Pane**.

8. Select the lower text box and apply an entrance effect of **Fly in**, choose **From Left** from **Direction**. Display the **Effect Options** and set to **Animate text All at once**.

9. To change the appearance of the text after it has been animated, from **After animation** drop down the list and select the colour **Blue**.

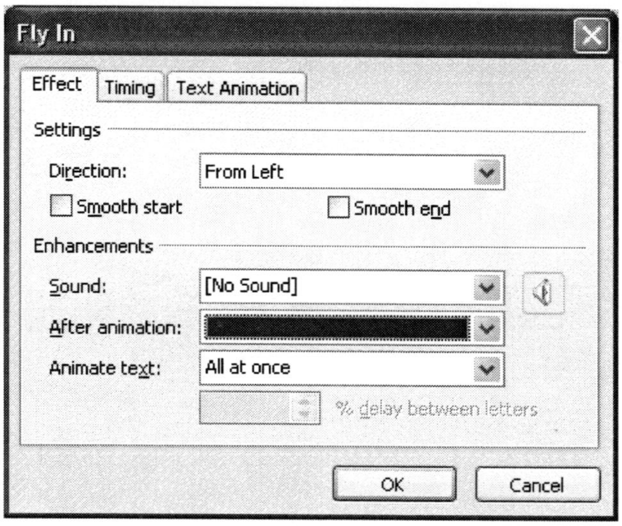

10. Click **OK**. Select the title text box and apply the **Swivel** entrance effect. **After animation** select the colour **White**.

11. To change the sequence of the animation effects just applied, move **Title 1** up to the top of the list.

12. View the slide show for slide **2** only, clicking the mouse to view the effects. The first click will introduce the title. At the next click the title will turn white, and the red bulleted list will appear. On the next mouse click the list turns blue.

13. End the show.

***Note:** You should produce evidence of the animation effects applied to slides.*

14. In **Normal View**, view slide **2** ensuring the **Custom Animation Task Pane** is displayed. Select **Title 1** and create a screen print of the animation effects applied to **Title 1**.

15. Open the **Evidence** document and paste in the screen print.

16. In the same way create a screen print of the animation effects applied to **Text 2**.

17. Enter suitable captions below the images. Save and close the document.

18. Save and close the presentation.

Exercise 36 - Animating Charts

Custom animation can be applied to charts. Available options include:

- How to introduce the chart elements
- Whether or not to animate the grid and legend
- Which animation effect and accompanying sound are applied
- What to do with the chart after it has been animated.

Activity:

1. Open the **Charts** presentation and in **Normal View**, select the chart by clicking on it once.
2. Select **Slide Show | Custom Animation** and apply the **Dissolve In** entrance effect.
3. Change the animation from **Dissolve** to **Blinds** with the **Direction** as **Horizontal** (you will need to **Remove** the previous effect from the **Task Pane**).
4. To change the way the chart elements are introduced, click on the **Chart 2** drop down arrow and select **Effect Options**. Select the **Chart Animation** tab and from **Group chart** select **By category**.

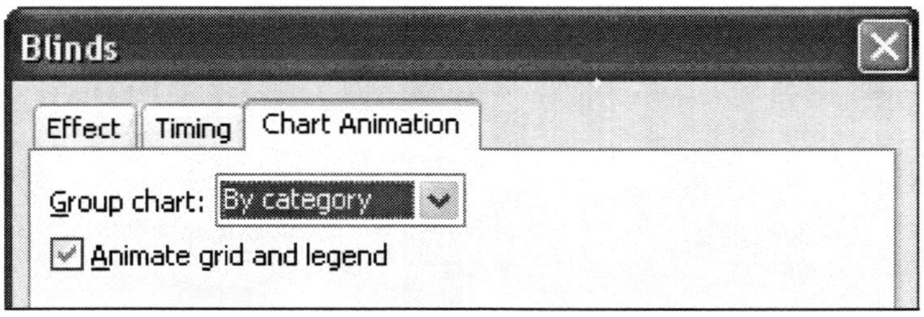

5. Click **OK** to return to the slide and view the slide show, clicking to introduce the chart elements.
6. Because of the chart type selected, the animation is not very effective. Double click on the chart and select **Chart | Chart Type**.
7. Select **Clustered column** and click **OK**.
8. View the show again, clicking to introduce the chart elements.
9. Save the presentation and close it.

> ***Note:*** *When a chart is imported from another application, for animation purposes it is classed as a picture frame. The options in the **Chart Effects** tab are ghosted out. Animation effects are applied to the chart as a whole from the **Effect** tab.*

Exercise 37 - Develop Your Skills

1. Open the **High Close** presentation and insert a **Blank** slide after slide **15**.

2. To improve your presentation and make it more interesting for the audience, you have decided to insert a video clip at the end. Click on the **Insert WordArt** button and from the **WordArt Gallery** select the second style from the left on row 4. Type **All Systems Go**.

3. Move the text to the top of the slide and increase the size. Change the character spacing to **Loose**.

4. From the supplied data insert the video clip called **launch**. Select to play automatically. Resize the movie clip to double its original size and move it below the title.

5. From the supplied data insert the sound file **apollo02**. Select to play it automatically. Drag the sound object on to the grey area surrounding the slide.

> ***Note:*** *The grey area surrounding the slide is called the* ***Gutter****. Any objects placed in the gutter area are not visible when the presentation is run.*

6. Set the order and timings and animation effects as follows:

   - Animation order **1 - WordArt**, **On click**, Effects **Checkerboard**, Builds (direction), **Across**.
   - Animation order **2 - sound**, **Start** automatically **With Previous**, **No effect**.
   - Animation order **3 - launch.mpeg**, **Start** automatically **With Previous**, **No effect**.

7. View the slide show for slide **16** only.

8. Move to slide **13 Gender Split**. Apply the timing and animation effects as follows:

   - Animation order **1 - Title 1**, **On mouse click**, Effects **Strips**, Builds (direction) **Left-Down**, Sound **Drum Roll**.
   - Animation order **2 - Chart 2**, **After Previous** - **3 seconds**, Chart Effects **Split**, Builds (direction) **Horizontal In**, introduce chart elements, **By element in series**.

9. View the slide show for slide **13** only.

10. Move to slide **2**, apply 2 different animation effects to the title and bulleted text. Start animation **On Click**.

11. Apply different animation effects to slide **4**.

12. View the slide show.

13. You should produce evidence showing the video clip object. Create a screen print of the **Insert Movie** dialog box for the video clip **launch** on slide **16**. Paste into the **Revision Evidence** document.

14. Create a screen print of the **Insert Sound** dialog box for the sound file **apollo02** and paste into the **Revision Evidence** document.

15. Create screen prints of the **Custom Animation Task Pane** displaying the different animation effects used for each of the slides.

16. Paste into the **Revision Evidence** document and enter suitable captions below the images.

17. Save and close the document. Close *Word.*

18. Save the presentation and close it.

Summary: Multimedia

Your ITQ evidence must demonstrate the following skills:

- Use a wide range of editing techniques to produce technically complex and interactive presentations. For example: cutting, rendering and exporting video clips; digitising and cutting sound clips from a microphone
- Check sound and moving images are edited appropriately
- Create interactive slides using time-line based tools
- Create new scenes using video editing software
- Play sound through a computer as part of a presentation.

You need to know and understand

- How to produce technically complex and interactive presentations. Technically complex and interactive presentations need to be produced using time-line based tools and may include sound and moving images
- How to include digitised sound and moving images, such as by recording sound through a computer, digitising sound from a microphone and capturing video
- What sound and image formats are suitable.

Read through the exercises in this Skill Set to give you some ideas of how you could demonstrate these skills.

Skill Set 5

Slide Shows

By the end of this Skill Set you should be able to:

Insert Slides
Hide Slides
Create a Custom Show
Run a Custom Show
Create and Edit Action Buttons
Use Hyperlinks
Apply Slide Transitions and Timings
Set up a Slide Show

Exercise 38 - Inserting Slides

Slides from existing presentations, sub presentations, or even whole presentations, can be imported into the current presentation.

Activity:

1. Open the **Progressive Training** presentation. In **Slide Sorter View** select slide **2**.

2. To import a slide, select **Insert | Slides from Files** to display the **Slide Finder** dialog box.

3. Click the **Browse** button and select the location of the data files from the **Look in** area of the **Browse** dialog box.

4. Select **The Company** presentation and click **Open**. The **Slide Finder** dialog box appears with the slides from the selected presentation shown in the **Select slides** area. Click on slide **2**.

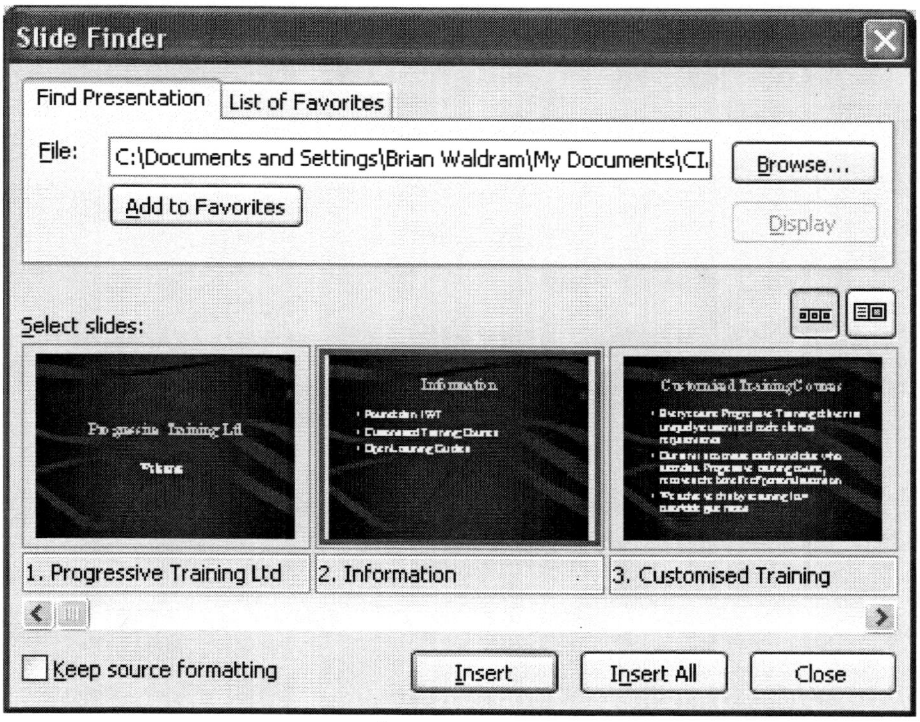

5. Click the **Insert** button to place the slide into the **Progressive Training** presentation. Close the **Slide Finder** dialog box. There may be a delay as the slide is changed to match the design of the **Progressive Training** presentation.

6. To insert more slides from a different presentation select slide **5** and then select **Insert | Slides from Files**. Select the **Extras** presentation from the data files and click **Open**.

7. Click **Insert All** to place all four slides of this presentation into **Progressive Training**.

8. Close the **Slide Finder** dialog box and view all twelve slides in the **Progressive Training** presentation.

9. Save the presentation and leave it open.

> ***Note:*** *You should produce evidence of slides which have been inserted from another presentation.*

10. Open the **Extras** presentation in **Slide Sorter View**. Create a screen print showing all slides from the **Extras** presentation.

11. Open the **Evidence** document and paste in the screen print.

12. Open **The Company** presentation and view slide **2** in **Normal View**. Create a screen print of the slide and paste in to the **Evidence** document.

13. Enter suitable captions below the images.

14. Save and close the document.

15. Close *Word.*

16. Close the **Extras** and **The Company** presentations.

Exercise 39 - Hiding Slides

Occasionally a presentation may have slides that contain sensitive information. If necessary these can be hidden.

Activity:

1. Open the **Progressive Training** presentation, if not open already from the previous exercise.

2. Select **View | Header and Footer**, check the box to include **Slide number** and click **Apply to All**.

3. The Director thinks the slide about training should be hidden. Make sure you are in **Slide Sorter View** and select slide **9**.

4. From the **Slide Sorter** toolbar click **Hide Slide**, . The symbol beneath the slide showing the slide number is altered to indicate that it will be hidden during the slide show.

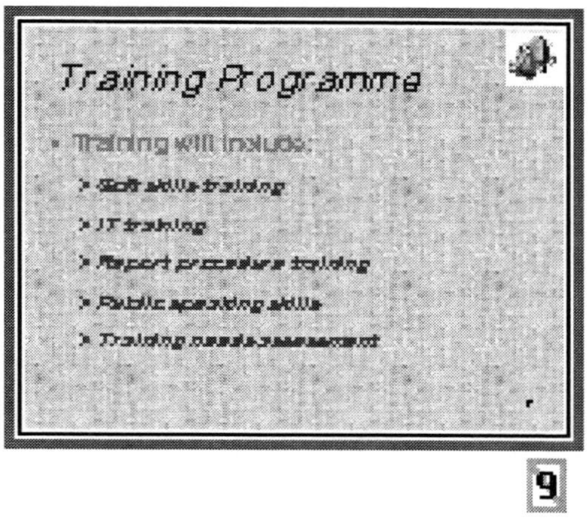

5. Select slide **1** and view the slide show.

6. Notice how slide **9** does not appear.

7. Save the presentation and close it.

Exercise 40 - Custom Shows

Custom shows allow different parts of one presentation to be shown as different shows to different audiences without the need for creating multiple versions of the same presentation. For example, an audience of salespeople could see a presentation without seeing those slides relating to administration and training, and finance staff could be given the same presentation but without the sales and training slides. A custom show can be set up so that certain slides can be missed out when necessary.

Activity:

1. Select **File | New** and select **From AutoContent Wizard** in the **New Presentation** task pane.

2. Click **Next** and then **Corporate** from **Presentation type**. **Business Plan** should be the default selection, if not select it and click **Next**.

3. Enter either your company name or your own name as a title where indicated and click **Finish**.

4. Save the presentation as **Custom Show**.

5. View the **Slides** pane in **Normal View**. The presentation is to be shown to two departments of the same company: **Finance** and **Marketing**. To avoid the creation of two separate presentations, two custom shows are to be created, each showing slightly different slides.

6. Select **Slide Show | Custom Shows** to display the **Custom Shows** dialog box, then click the **New** button to open the **Define Custom Show** dialog box.

7. Name the custom show **Finance** as this is the show to be given to that department.

8. The **Finance** staff do not need to see all of the **Marketing** slides. Select the first slide, then click **Add**.

9. Select slide **2** and then hold down **<Ctrl>** as you select slides **4**, **9**, **11** and **12**. Click **Add** to add them to the custom show, then click **OK** to return to the **Custom Shows** dialog box.

10. Create another custom show called **Marketing** (slides **1**, **2**, **3**, **4**, **6**, **7** and **12**). Click **OK**.

11. To edit the **Marketing** department's show, select **Marketing** from the list in the **Custom Shows** dialog box.

12. Click **Edit**. Slide **5** is to be removed.

13. Click on slide **5 Business Concept** at the right of the dialog box.

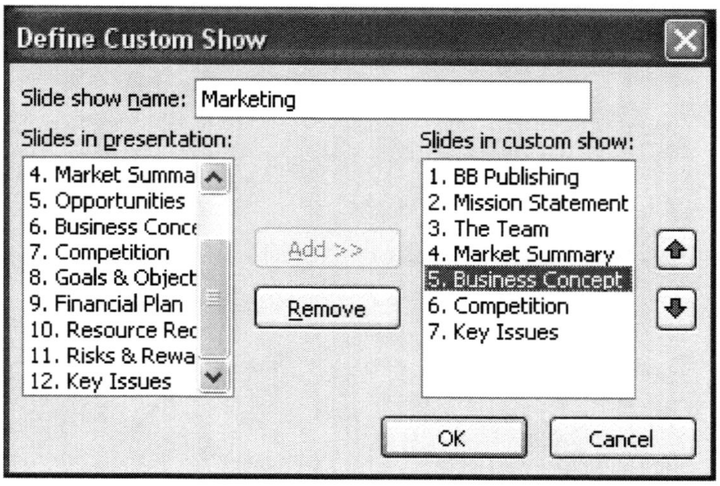

14. Click **Remove**.

15. Slide **4 Market Summary** is to be moved after **Competition**. Select slide **4** from the right of the dialog box.

16. Click **Move Down**, .

17. Click **OK** and then **Close**.

18. Save the presentation as **Custom Show** and leave it open.

Exercise 41 - Running a Custom Show

After custom shows have been created they can be run via the menus, or more professionally by adding action buttons to the presentation.

Activity:

1. View slide **1** of the **Custom Show** presentation in **Normal View** and select **Slide Show | Custom Shows**.
2. To run the **Finance** show, select it from the list.

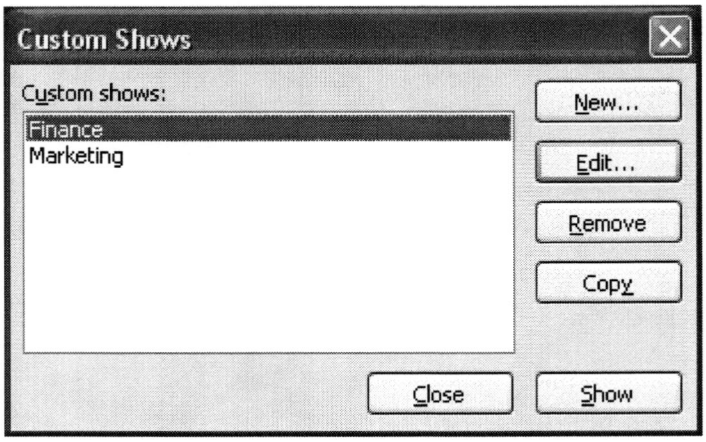

3. Click **Show**.
4. Click the mouse to advance the slides, noting which slides are displayed, and click to exit.
5. View the **Marketing** show in the same way.

Note: *You should produce evidence of the custom shows.*

6. Select **Slide Show | Custom Shows**, select the **Finance** show, click **Edit** to display the **Define Custom Show** dialog box. Create a screen print of the **Finance** custom show.
7. Open the **Evidence** document and paste in the screen print.
8. In the same way, create a screen print of the **Marketing** custom show and paste into the **Evidence** document.
9. Insert suitable captions below both images.
10. Save and close the document. Close *Word.*
11. Save the presentation and leave it open.

Exercise 42 - Action Buttons

Action buttons can be added to allow rapid and easy navigation between slides during the presentation. Action buttons also allow movement to other presentations, files, web sites and various other destinations.

Activity:

1. Open the **Custom Show** presentation, if not open already from the previous exercise.

2. It would be better to select the required show by using action buttons on the first slide. To create an action button on slide **1**, click the **AutoShapes** button, 

, on the **Drawing** toolbar.

3. Select **Action Buttons** and then select the **Custom** action button, .

4. Click and drag the shape of the button on the bottom left side of the slide.

5. In the **Action Settings** dialog box, select **Hyperlink to** and from the list select **Custom Show** and select **Finance** then click **OK**.

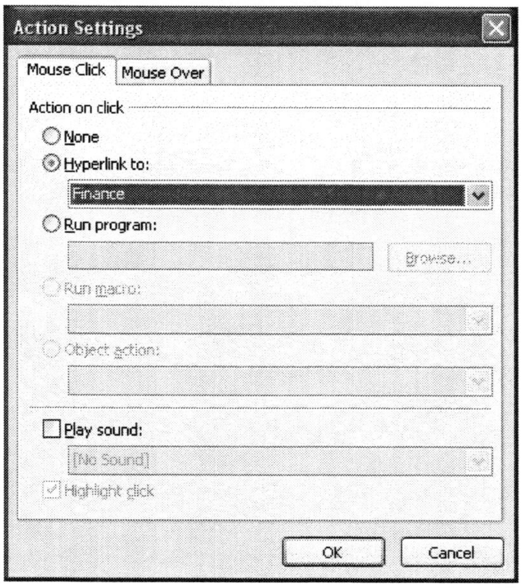

6. Click **OK** again. With the button selected type **Finance** to label it. Click away from the button.

7. Repeat the above steps to create a button for the **Marketing** custom show on the bottom right of the slide.

8. Resize and move the buttons as necessary.

9. Because slide **1** will now always be displayed before you start the custom shows, you may want to remove slide 1 from each custom show sequence. To remove slide **1**, select **Slide Show | Custom Shows**, select the **Finance** show and click the **Edit** button.

10. Select slide **1** from the list on the right and click **Remove**. Click **OK**. Repeat these steps for the **Marketing** show, then close the **Custom Shows** dialog box.

11. Run the full slide show (12 slides) and then start the slide show again and use the **Finance** button to see that custom show, advancing by clicking. This is easier than using the menus. Notice the slide numbers at the bottom right.

12. Run the slide show again and use the **Marketing** button to see that custom show.

13. Save the **Custom Show** presentation and close it.

14. Open the **IT Training** presentation and save it as **IT Training1**.

15. In **Normal View** move to slide **4**, title **The Open Learning Guide**.

16. To create an action button that links to slide **7**, click the **AutoShapes** button, then **Action Buttons** select the **Information** action button, .

17. Click and drag the shape of the button on to the bottom left side of the slide.

***Note:** If a message appears about saving the presentation, select **Yes**.*

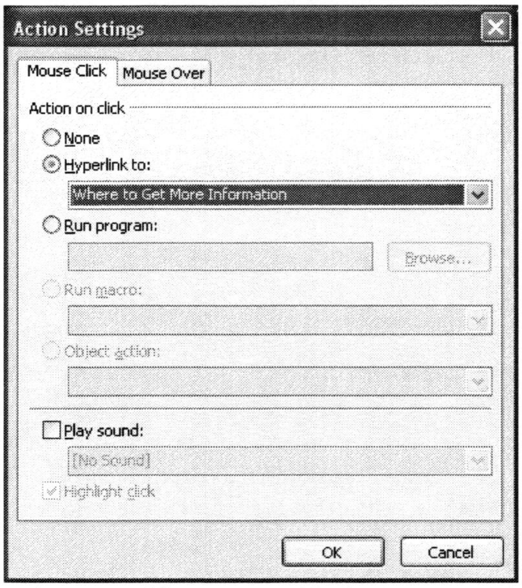

18. The **Action Settings** dialog box appears. Ensure that the **Mouse Click** tab is selected.

19. Click the **Hyperlink to** option and from the drop down list, select **Slide**, then from the list of slides displayed, select slide **7 Where to Get More Information**.

20. Click **OK**. Click **OK** again.

21. Click the **Slide Show** button to see the slide as it will appear in the presentation.

22. When the cursor appears, click the action button. The presentation moves to the **Where to Get More Information** slide. Read the details and then press <**Esc**>.

23. To create a link from slide **7** back to slide **4** so that the presentation can continue to run in the correct sequence, draw a **Back or Previous** action button, , at the bottom right on slide **7**.

24. From **Action Settings** select **Hyperlink to Slide**.

25. From **Hyperlink to Slide**, select slide **4 The Open Learning Guide**.

26. Click **OK** and **OK** again.

27. Run the show from slide **1**, clicking the mouse to advance the show. Click the action button on slide **4** to hyperlink to slide **7**, then click the **Back or Previous** action button on slide **7** to return to slide **4**.

28. Press <**Esc**> to end the show and return to **Normal View**.

29. At the bottom left of slide **5** draw a **Document** action button, . This will link to a *Word* document.

30. From **Action Settings** select **Hyperlink to | Other File**.

31. Choose the **Sample** file and click **OK** then **OK** again. Enter **Sample file** as the name of the action button, resizing if necessary.

32. Run the show and after the text has loaded click the button. *Word* starts and opens the document.

33. Close *Word* and end the show.

34. Move to slide **7**. Draw a custom action button at the bottom left of the slide.

35. From **Hyperlink to**, select **URL**. Type in the following address:

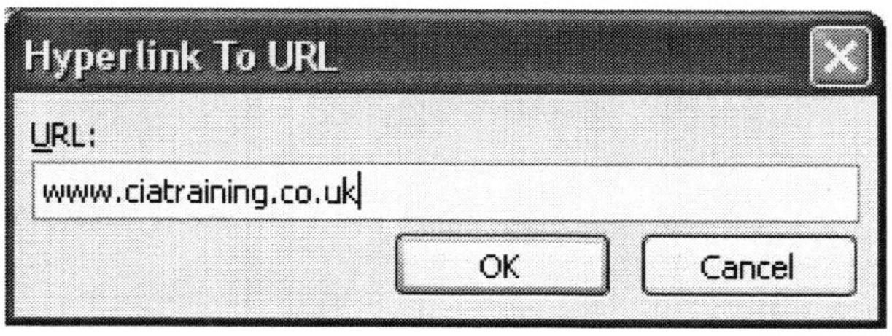

36. Click **OK** and **OK** again.

37. With the button selected, type **CiA Web**.

38. Resize the button to fit the text.

39. Run the show and click the action button. Your browser application will start and if a connection exists the button will open the **CiA** home page.

40. Close the browser and end the show. Save the **IT Training1** presentation and leave it open.

Exercise 43 - Editing an Action Button

It is possible to change the destination of an action button after creating it. This may be necessary if a web address (**URL**) or a file location changes.

Activity:

1. With the presentation **IT Training1** in **Normal View**, view slide **7**.
2. Right click on the edge of the **CiA Web** button (not on the text content).and select **Edit Hyperlink**. The current hyperlink destination is shown.

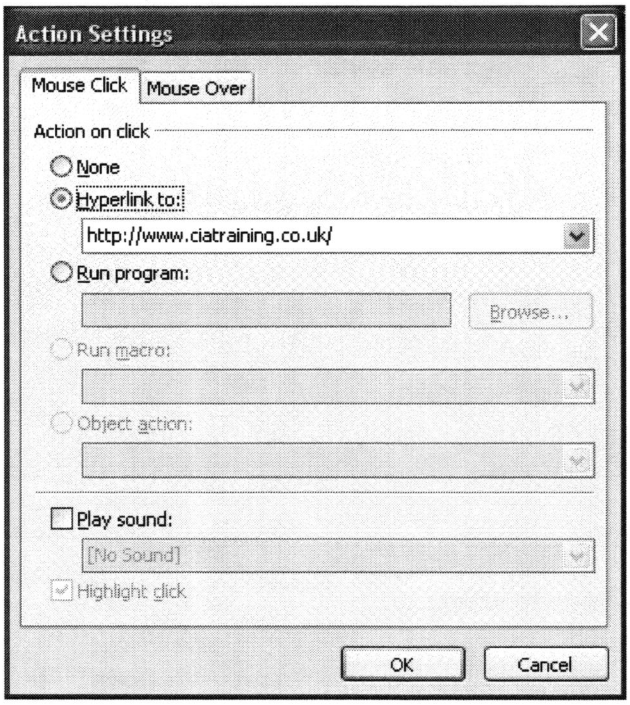

3. Drop down the **Hyperlink to** list and select **URL**.
4. To link to a different web page change the address in **Hyperlink to URL** to **www.itq.e-skills.com** and click **OK**, then click **OK** again in the **Action Settings** dialog box.
5. Change the text on the button to **OCR** by double clicking on the text and overtyping.

Note: *Any action button can have its destination changed in this way, whether it's to a slide, a presentation, a file, URL, etc.*

6. If you have an Internet connection, run the show and click the button when the text has loaded.
7. View the site then close the browser and end the show.
8. Save the presentation and leave it open.

Exercise 44 - Using Hyperlinks in Slides

Hyperlinks are text or images which move directly to another location when they are clicked. Previous exercises have covered hyperlinks as actions on buttons, but they can also be added to any object on a slide. Hyperlinks to other slides in a presentation, to other files, to an **E-mail** address, to a location on an **Intranet**, or on the **Internet** can easily be created.

Activity:

1. Open the presentation **IT Training1**, if not open already from the previous exercise.

2. On slide **7**, select the text **info@ciatraining.co.uk** and click **Insert Hyperlink**, . The **Insert Hyperlink** dialog box is displayed.

3. Select the **E-mail Address** button, 

, if not already selected.

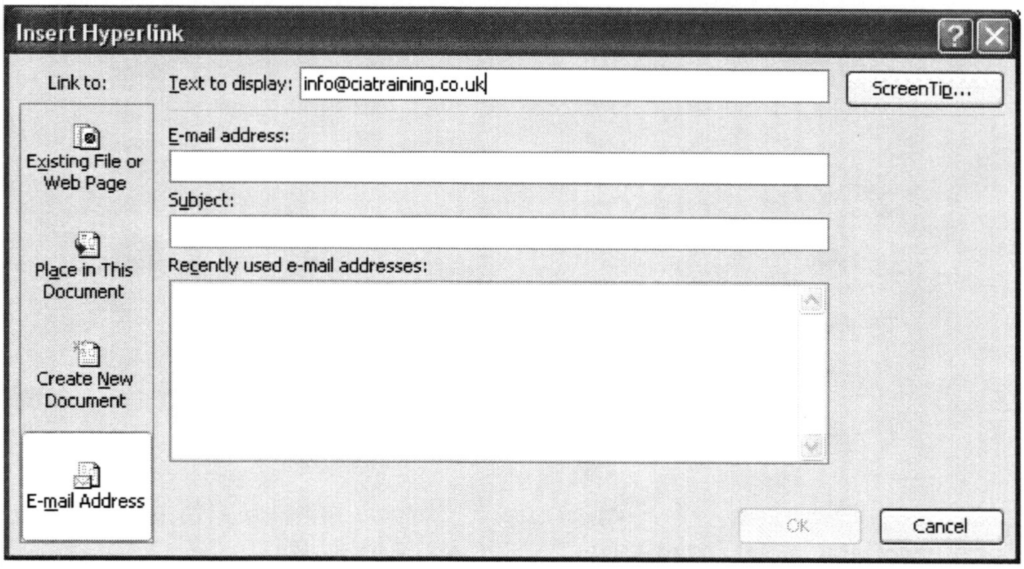

> **Note:** *Hyperlinks to Web pages or existing files can be created by clicking* 
>
> *, then typing the web or file address, or by browsing for it.*

4. Type the following address, **info@ciatraining.co.uk** in the **E-mail address** box. Click **OK**.

5. View the slide show for this slide.

6. Move the mouse pointer over the e-mail address. The pointer changes to a hand shape.

Note: *When an e-mail address is typed on a slide, the hyperlink is created automatically. Any text with a hyperlink applied will be a different colour to other text on the slide. When the hyperlink destination has been visited, the text colour changes.*

7. Click on the **e-mail address**. An untitled message opens in your e-mail application. This example uses *Microsoft Outlook.*

Note: *If Word is set up as the e-mail editor, this program will start instead and the message will look slightly different.*

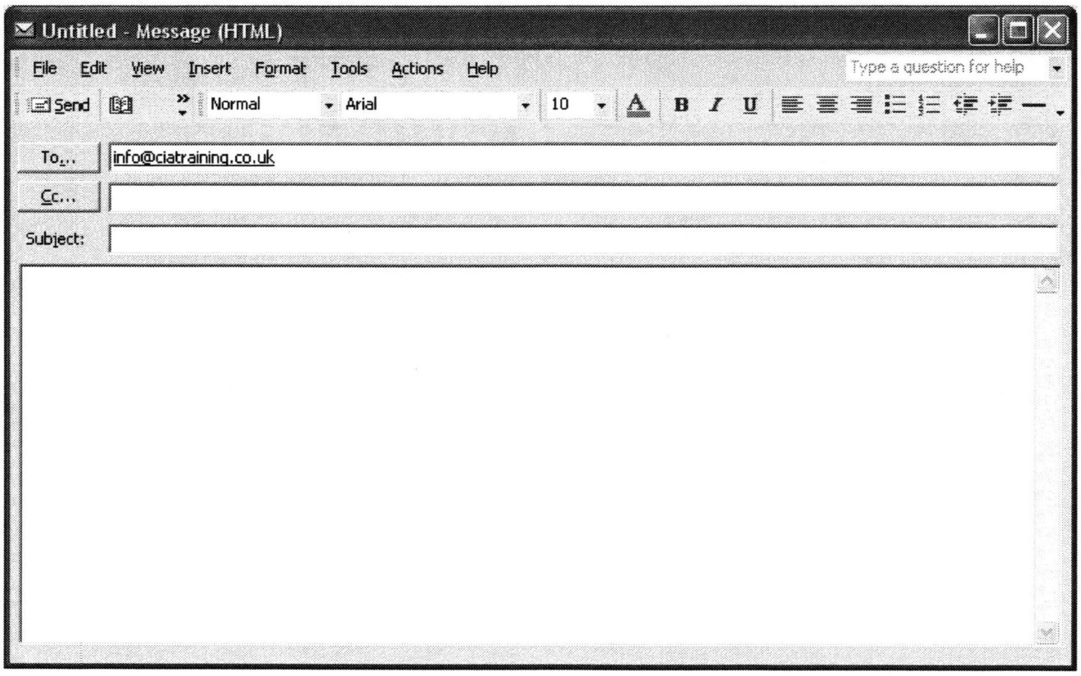

8. The cursor should be flashing in the subject box. Type **More Information** for the subject. Click in the message box and type **Please send me details of ITQ Level 3 products**.

9. If you click **Send**, the message would be sent, but in this instance you are not sending the message. However, you need to produce evidence of the link to an e-mail address. Create a screen print.

10. Close the untitled message dialog box. Click **No** to the message prompt. *Microsoft Outlook* closes.

Note: *If Word has been opened, select **File | Exit** and do <u>not</u> save.*

11. End the slide show.

12. Open the **Evidence** document and paste in the screen print.

13. Enter a suitable caption below the image.

14. Save and leave the document open.

15. Return to the **IT Training1** presentation.

16. Move to slide **4**, right click on the **Information** action button.

17. Select **Edit Hyperlink** to display the current hyperlink destination. Create a screen print of the hyperlink.

18. Return to the **Evidence** document and paste in the screen print.

19. Move to slide **7**, and right click on the **OCR** action button.

20. Select **Edit Hyperlink** to display the current hyperlink destination. Create a screen print of the hyperlink.

21. Return to the **Evidence** document and paste in the screen print.

22. Create a screen print of the hyperlink destination of the action button on slide **5**, and paste in to the **Evidence** document.

23. Close *Word,* saving the document.

24. Save the presentation and close it.

Exercise 45 - Applying Transitions

To add interest to a slide show, a transition can be applied to slides. This is a special effect, which controls how one slide changes to the next. Timings can be applied to the effects, so that they appear after a specified interval, or they can be displayed manually by clicking the mouse.

Activity:

1. Open the **Custom Show** presentation and change the view to **Slide Sorter View**.
2. To create a transition effect, select slide **1** and click the **Slide Transition** button, Transition. The **Slide Transition Task Pane** appears.

> **Note:** *The **Slide Transition** button is only found on the **Slide Sorter** toolbar in **Slide Sorter View**, but the task pane can be displayed in other views by selecting **Slide Show | Slide Transition**.*

3. A list of transition effects is shown at the top of the **Task Pane**. Use the scroll bar to see the available effects.

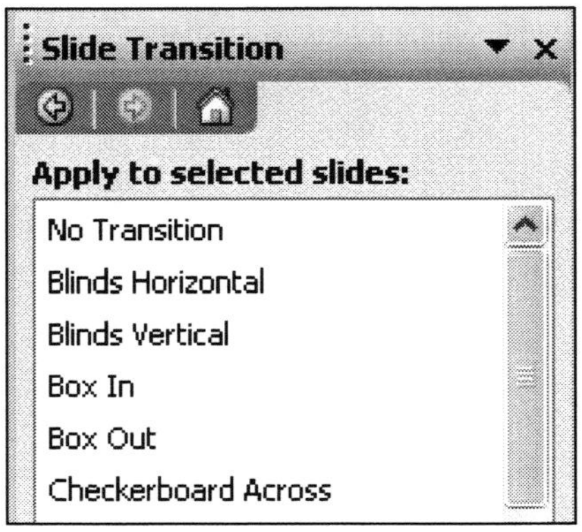

4. Pick any one. A demonstration of the effect is shown.
5. Try using some of the other effects to see what they do, then select **Dissolve**.
6. From **Modify transition** select the speed **Medium** and from **Advance slide** ensure **On mouse click** is selected, then click **Apply to All Slides**. All slides now have the **Dissolve** transition effect applied.

> **Note:** *A slide that has a transition or animation applied has a symbol underneath it in **Slide Sorter View**.*

> **Note:** *Each slide can have a different effect if desired, although normally they would all be the same. Select the slide, choose an effect from the* ***Slide Transition Task Pane****. Repeat for each slide.*

7. Select slide **1**, then view the slide show.

8. Click the mouse button to move through all the slides and notice the effects as the slides change.

9. At the moment the effects do not appear until the mouse is clicked. To apply timings to the transition effect select slide **1** in **Slide Sorter View**.

10. Click in **On mouse click** in the **Slide Transition** task pane to remove the check, then check **Automatically after**.

11. Use the up spinner to increase the time to **5** seconds:

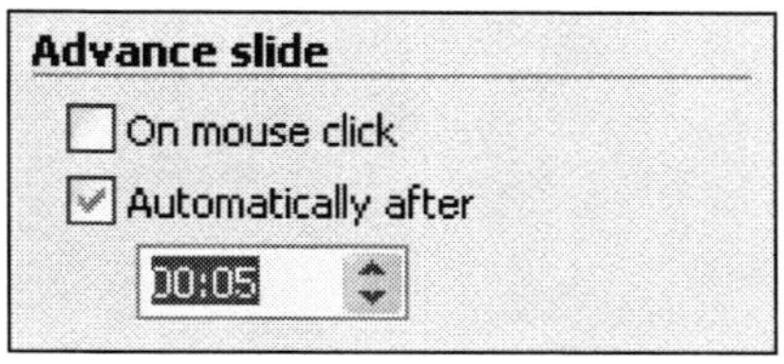

12. Click **Apply to All Slides**. The transition timing for each slide is now shown underneath the slide image in **Slide Sorter View**.

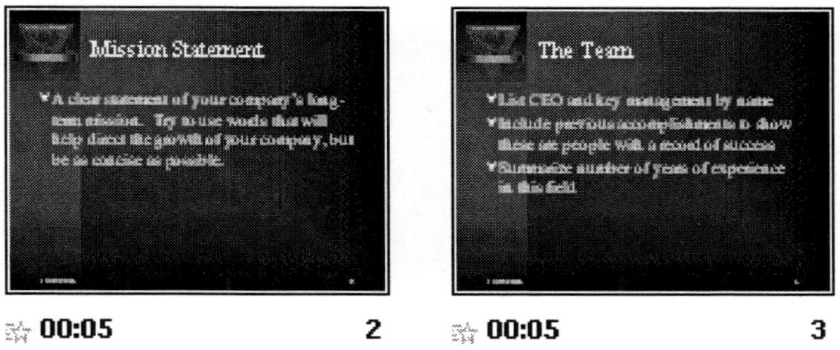

13. View the slide show without clicking the mouse. Using this option the slide show could be left to run without the need for a presenter, as a continuously running display for example.

> **Note:** *If the slide show does not run, select* ***Slide Show | Set Up Show*** *and ensure that* ***Using timings if present*** *is selected under* ***Advance Slides****.*

14. When the show ends, change the settings back for all slides so the transitions are activated when the mouse is clicked.

> **Note:** *It is possible to select both* ***Advance*** *options (mouse click and automatic) at the same time. Then each transition can be activated by using the mouse if required, but if this is not used within the set time, the transition will start automatically.*

15. Save the presentation.

> **Note:** *You should produce evidence of the transition effects applied to slides.*

16. In **Slide Sorter View**, change the zoom to **50%**.
17. Display the **Slide Transition Task Pane** if not already displayed.
18. Create a screen print of the slides with the transition symbol displayed below.
19. Open the **Evidence** document and paste in the screen print.
20. Enter a suitable caption below the image.
21. Save and close the document. Close *Word*.
22. Leave the presentation open.

Exercise 46 - Applying Timings

As an alternative to applying timings to transitions, usually for looped presentations, timings can be applied to each individual slide allowing the presenter to describe each before it is advanced. These are set up during a **Rehearsal**.

> **Note:** *If a presentation contains hyperlinks and action buttons it should be run manually, so that the links can be used.*

Activity:

1. Open the **Custom Show** presentation, if not open already from the previous exercise.

2. In **Slide Sorter View**, select the first slide and to apply timings click the **Rehearse Timings** button, (in other views, select **Slide Show | Rehearse Timings**). The slide show begins, with the **Rehearsal** dialog box on the screen.

3. Allow enough time to talk about the slide then click the **Next** button, . The next screen appears with the time for the current slide reset to zero.

4. Pause the rehearsal by clicking , then restart it using the same button. Move to the next slide/effect.

5. View the entire presentation, clicking the **Next** button after the required time period for each slide until finished.

6. At the end of the rehearsal a dialog box appears showing the total time for the slide show and asking if the timings are to be saved for future use.

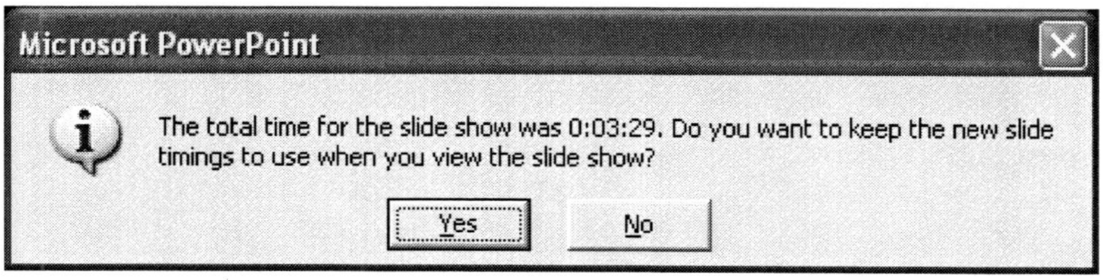

7. To produce evidence of rehearsed timings, create a screen print before you click **Yes**,

8. Click **Yes**. The individual times for each slide are now displayed. The total time for the slide show is made up of these times. The timing can be changed at any time by clicking the **Rehearse Timings** button again.

9. Individual timings can still be amended. Select slide **3** and in the **Task Pane** increase the time value by 5 seconds.

10. Save the presentation and leave it open.

11. Open the **Evidence** document and paste in the screen print, showing the total time of the slide show.

12. Switch to the **Custom Show** presentation.

13. In **Slide Sorter View**, create a screen print of the timings applied to all slides.

14. Open the **Evidence** document and paste in the screen print.

15. Insert suitable captions below the image.

16. Save and close the document. Close *Word*.

17. Leave the presentation open.

Exercise 47 - Setting up a Slide Show

A slide show can be set up to run in a few different ways. It can be run manually, by clicking the mouse, or automatically using timings. It can also be set up to loop, running continuously. Even when timings have been applied to a show, you should check to make sure that it has been set up to use these timings.

Activity:

1. Open the **Custom Show** presentation, if not open already from the previous exercise.

2. To make sure the timings specified earlier are to be used when the show runs, in **Slide Sorter View**, select **Slide Show | Set Up Show**.

3. In the **Set Up Show** dialog box, under **Advance slides**, select the option for **Using timings, if present**.

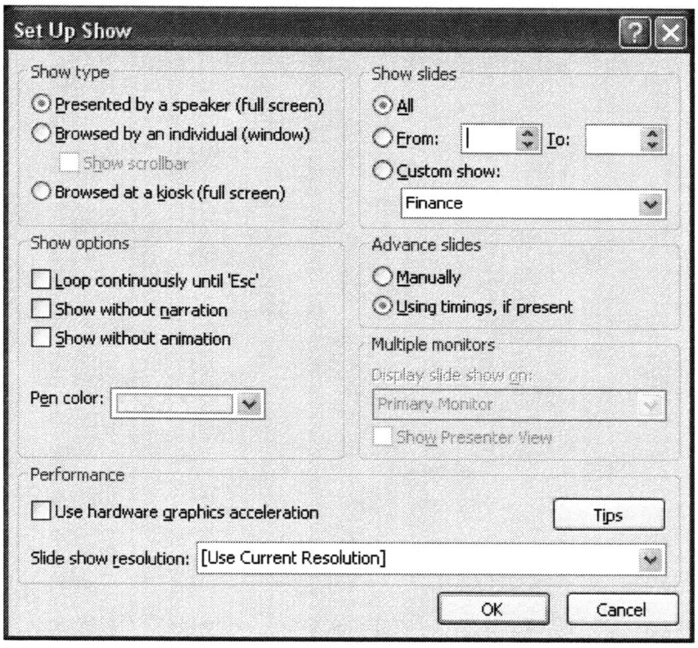

4. Click **OK**, then save the presentation. View the slide show, which will now play using the timings set in the rehearsal. There is no need to click the mouse.

5. At the end of the show *PowerPoint* returns to **Slide Sorter View**. Select **Slide Show | Set Up Show**.

6. To ignore the timings select **Advance slides Manually**. Click **OK**.

7. Select slide **1** and then view the show.

8. The first slide in the presentation appears. Click the mouse to move to the second slide.

9. Move through the rest of the slide show.

10. At the end of the show *PowerPoint* returns to **Slide Sorter View**. Change the set up to use timings again using the **Set Up Show** dialog box, but don't click **OK** yet.

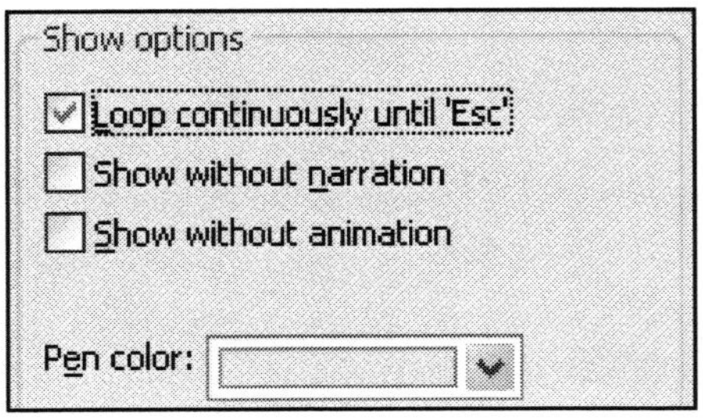

11. To make the show run continuously, check **Loop continuously until 'Esc'**.

12. Click **OK**. View the show and when the end is reached, the show will start again.

13. Press <**Esc**> to end the slide show.

14. To stop the show looping, select **Slide Show | Set Up Show** and uncheck **Loop continuously....**

15. Click **OK**.

16. Save and close the presentation.

17. Open the **Holidays2** presentation.

18. Remove the current effect from the picture on slide **1**.

19. Apply custom animation, the **Fly In** effect, direction **From Left**, to the picture on slide **1**, to start **3** seconds **After Previous** event.

20. View the show for this slide only.

21. The show can also be run without animation. Select **Slide Show | Set Up Show**.

22. Check **Show without animation** and click **OK**.

23. View the show for this slide again and notice how neither the picture nor the **WordArt** are animated.

24. Close the presentation without saving.

Exercise 48 - Develop Your Skills

1. Open the presentation **High Close** in **Slide Sorter View**.

2. With slide **14** selected, import all slides from the presentation **General Information**.

3. You have been asked to produce a short version of your presentation which is to be shown to all casual staff. Create a new custom show called **Brief**. Add the slides **Recommendations**, **New Organisation Structure**, **Market Research**, **Market Research - Analysis**, and **High Close FE College**.

4. You should produce evidence of the imported slides and custom show. Open the **General Information** presentation in **Slide Sorter View**. Create a screen print of all slides.

5. Open the **Revision Evidence** document and paste in the screen print.

6. Enter a suitable caption, for example, **Screen print of 3 slides imported from General Information presentation. See imported slides in main presentation on page xx below the image.**

7. Display the **Define Custom Show** dialog box. Create a screen print and paste in to the **Revision Evidence** document.

8. Save the document and leave it open.

9. Leave the **High Close** presentation open, but close **General Information** without saving.

> ***Note:*** *For this revision exercise, 2 sub presentations have already been created called **Business Faculty** and **IT faculty**.*

10. View slide **14**, **Market Research - Analysis**. Draw a **Custom** action button at the bottom left of the slide. Create a link to the **Business Faculty** presentation hyperlinking to slide **1**. Call the action button **Business**.

11. Draw a second **Custom** action button on slide **14** at the bottom right of the slide. Create a link to the **IT faculty** presentation hyperlinking to slide **1**. Call the action button **IT** and save the presentation.

12. Open the **Business Faculty** presentation.

13. Move to slide **3**. Draw a **Back or Previous** action button at the bottom right of the slide. Create a link back to slide **14** in the **High Close** presentation.

14. Open the **IT faculty** presentation and repeat step **13**.

15. Run the slide show for slide **14** only of the **High Close** presentation, to test the hyperlink which runs the **Business Faculty** sub presentation. This will be displayed when the presentation is shown to the Business staff. Test the link on the sub presentation; it should link back to slide **14** so that the presentation can run in the correct sequence.

16. Run the slide show again for slide **14**, to test the hyperlinks to and from the **IT faculty** sub presentation. End any running slide shows.

17. You have decided that slide, **9 Funding** may not be relevant to all staff and should be hidden. Hide slide **9**.

18. Draw a custom action button on slide **15**. Create a hyperlink to the hidden slide, **9 Funding**. Name the action button **Funding**.

19. Draw **Back or Previous** action button on slide **9**. Create a hyperlink back to slide **15**. Run the slide show for slide **15** only, to test the hyperlinks.

20. You should produce evidence of the links to the sub presentations and links back to the main presentation. Display the **Action Settings** dialog box for the **Business** action button, by right clicking on the border of the button and selecting **Action Settings**. Create a screen print and paste in to the **Revision Evidence** document.

21. Create screen prints of all the action buttons and paste them in to the **Revision Evidence** document. Enter a suitable caption below each image.

22. Save the document and leave it open.

23. Close both sub presentations, saving the changes. Save and leave the **High Close** presentation open.

24. Move to slide **18**. Insert the slide, **More Information** from the presentation named **Web site**.

25. Select the text **www.dfes.gov.uk** and create a hyperlink to that web page.

26. Create a hyperlink to **www.lsc.gov.uk** and **info@lsc.gov.uk**.

27. You should produce evidence of the hyperlinks. Create screen prints of the **Edit Hyperlink** dialog box for each hyperlink and paste in to the **Revision Evidence** document.

28. Modify the hyperlink **www.lsc.gov.uk** to **www.lsc.gov.uk/contactus.cfm**.

29. Create a screen print of the modified hyperlink and paste in to the **Revision Evidence** document.

30. Move to slide **6**, select the title **Retention Rates**. Create a hyperlink to **Data for 1998-2002.xls** file: select **Existing File or Web Page**, from **Look in** select the data folder and then select the file.

31. You should produce evidence of editing the hyperlinks. On slide **6**, right click on the text **Retention Rates**. Select **Edit Hyperlink** to display the current hyperlink destination.

32. Create a screen print of the **Open** dialog box showing the file **Data for 1998-2002.xls** in its original location. Paste into **Revision Evidence**.

33. Move to slide **19**, select the title text, **More Information**. Create a hyperlink to the **LSC News.doc** file.

34. Create a screen print of the file **LSC News.doc** as in steps **31** and **32** and paste in to the **Revision Evidence** document.

35. Save the **Revision Evidence** document and leave it open.

36. In **Slide Sorter View**, apply the slide transition effect **Box In** to slide numbers **1** to **4**. Apply the transition effect **Box Out** to slide numbers **5** to **8**. Apply the transition effect **Cover Down** to slide numbers **9** to **14** and the transition effect **Cover Left** to slide numbers **15** to **20**.

37. Create a screen print of the **Slide Transition Task Pane** displaying each slide transition effect, that is shown beneath the **Add Effect** button

38. In **Slide Sorter View** click the **Rehearse Timings** button. Allow enough time to talk about each slide.

39. Set the show up to run using timings.

40. At the end of the rehearsal, create a screen print of the **Rehearsal** dialog box and paste in to the **Revision Evidence** document.

41. Create a screen print of timings applied to all slides.

42. Save the presentation and close any open presentations.

43. Save the **Revision Evidence** document and close it.

Summary: Slide Shows

Your ITQ evidence must demonstrate the following skills:

- Make references to external data. For example: hyperlinks, object linking and embedding
- Rehearse and check timing of a slide show
- Format technically complex and interactive presentations using appropriate tools and techniques. For example: creating a master slide to format consistently; using different formats in each section and creating different slide transitions
- Create interactive slides using time-line based tools
- Play sound through a computer as part of a presentation.

You need to know and understand

- How to produce technically complex and interactive presentations. Technically complex and interactive presentations need to be produced using time-line based tools and may include sound and moving images

Read through the exercises in this Skill Set to give you some ideas of how you could demonstrate these skills.

Skill Set 6

Macros

By the end of this Skill Set you should be able to:

Record A Macro
Run A Macro
Record A Multiple Action Macro
Assign Macros to a Button and Menu

Exercise 49 - Recording a Macro

Macros are used to save time. They are composed of a series of recorded actions that can then be run in sequence.

With more and more viruses being attached to macros, security has become an issue. *Microsoft Office* products include a comprehensive security system to control the use of macros. The system is based on three levels of security: **high**, **medium** and **low**. The effect of the security level settings also depends on what type of digital signature, if any, has been attached to the macros. The assignment of digital signatures is beyond the scope of this guide. Macros in this guide have no signatures and will not work with a **High** level of security active.

Activity:

1. Open the **Progressive Training** presentation. A macro is to be set up to print handouts (sometimes called **Thumbnails**).

2. To check the macro security, select **Tools | Macro | Security**. On the **Security Level** tab note the current setting so it can be reset later.

3. Read the description for each level, then select **Medium**. Click **OK**.

4. In **Slide Sorter View**, select **Tools | Macro | Record New Macro**.

5. In **Macro Name** enter **Handouts** and make sure **Store macro in** shows **Progressive Training.ppt**.

6. Click **OK** and follow the next instructions precisely, as the macro is recording.

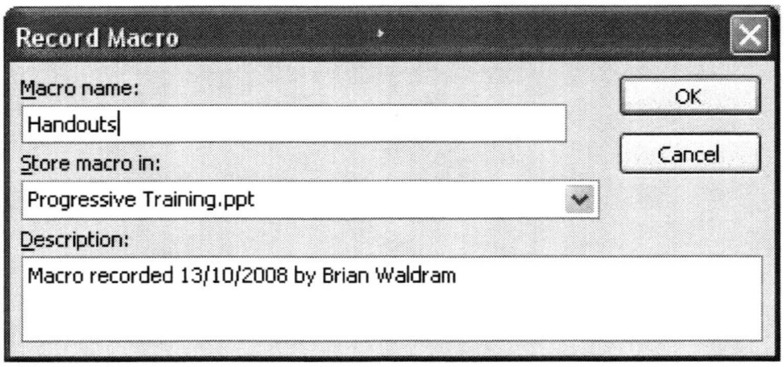

7. Select **File | Print**, from the **Print what** drop down list, select **Handouts**.

8. From the drop down list next to **Slides per page**, select **3**.

9. The small preview at the right shows how the print out will appear. Click **OK**.

10. Click the **Stop Recording** button, ▪. The macro **Handouts** has now been recorded.

> **Note:** *If the **Stop Recording** toolbar is not visible, right click on a toolbar and select **Stop Recording**. Or, use **Tools | Macro | Stop Recording**.*

11. Save the presentation as **Macro** and leave it open.

Exercise 50 - Running a Macro

Macros can be run by using standard menu options. Later exercises will show how they can be assigned to customised buttons or menus.

Activity:

1. Open the **Macro** presentation, if not open already from the previous exercise.

2. To apply the macro created earlier, select **Tools | Macro | Macros** from the menu.

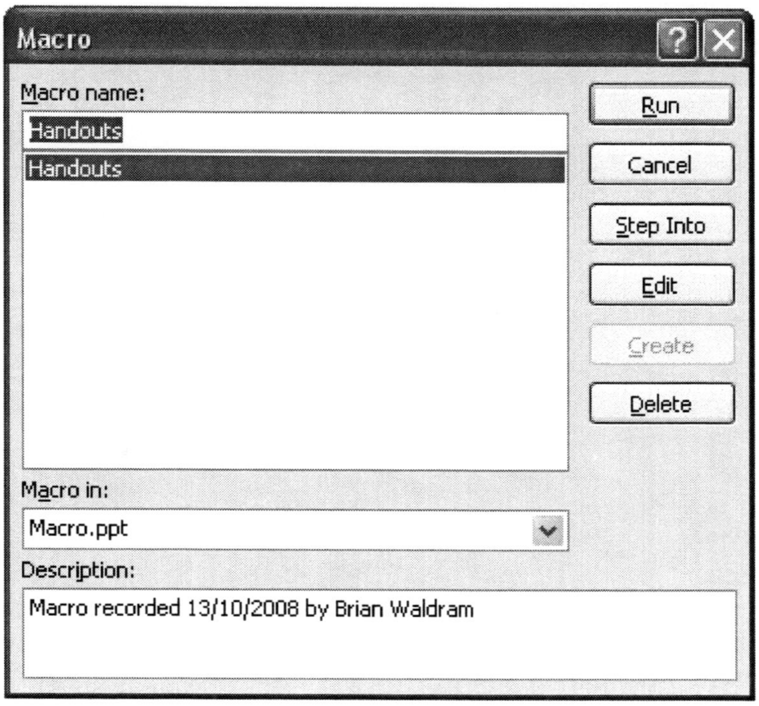

3. The **Handouts** macro is shown in the dialog box. Make sure it is selected and click **Run**. The handouts are printed, 3 slides per page.

4. Leave the presentation **Macro** open.

Exercise 51 - Multiple Action Macros

Macros can be recorded to perform a sequence of tasks, such as saving and printing a presentation.

Activity:

1. Open the presentation **Macro**, if not open already from the previous exercise. A macro is to be set up to save the presentation and then print it.

2. In **Normal View**, select **Tools | Macro | Record New Macro**.

3. In **Macro name** enter **SavePrint** and make sure **Store macro in** shows **Macro.ppt**.

4. Click **OK** and follow the next instructions precisely.

5. Select **File | Save**.

6. Select **File | Print** leave the default option as **All**, click **OK**.

7. Click the **Stop Recording** button.

8. Save the presentation and leave it open.

9. Run the **SavePrint** macro to save the presentation and print all slides.

10. Leave the presentation open for the next exercise.

Exercise 52 - Assigning a Macro

The **Customize** dialog box can be used to assign a macro to a button on a toolbar. The button can then be added to any toolbar and its appearance can also be changed. A macro can also be assigned to the **Menu Bar** as a new menu.

> ***Note:*** *In some applications a* ***Keyboard shortcut*** *can be assigned to a macro, however this is not possible in PowerPoint 2003.*

Activity:

1. Open the **Macro** presentation, if not open already from the previous exercise.

2. In **Normal View**, select **Tools | Customize**.

3. From the **Commands** tab, scroll down the **Categories** list and select **Macros**.

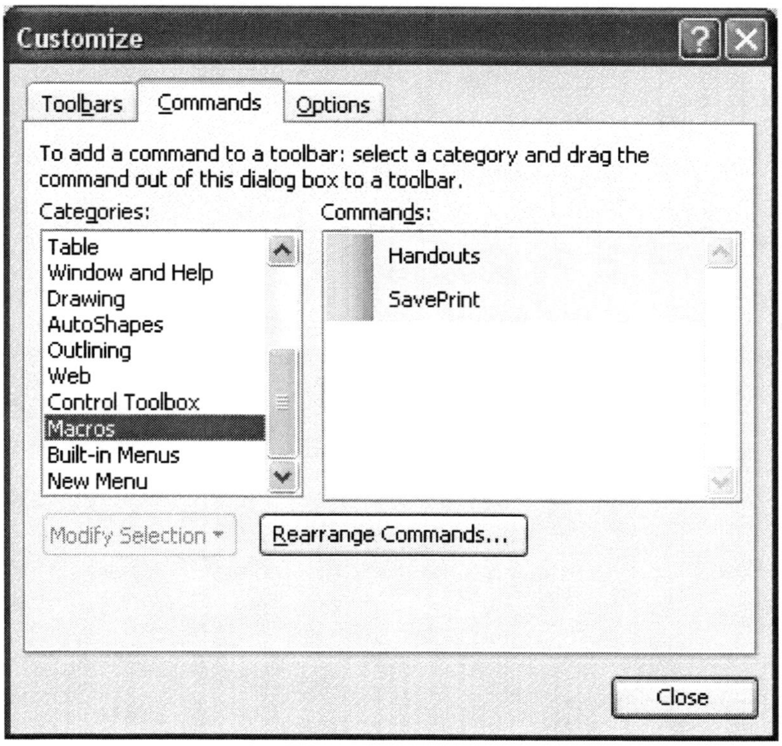

4. The macro **Handouts** is shown at the right of the dialog box. Click on it and hold down the mouse button.

5. Drag the command button on to the **Standard Toolbar**, 

, and release the button.

6. Now click **Modify Selection** in the dialog box and in **Name** delete the text and type in **Print handouts**.

> **Note:** *The button can be changed to a picture by clicking **Change Button Image** and selecting from the options displayed. Choosing **Default Style** will show the image only.*

7. Close the dialog box. Notice how the button has changed, 

.

8. Click, 

, to run the macro.

> **Note:** *Remove a customised button (or menu) by holding <**Alt**> and dragging it down off the toolbar (or menu bar). To delete a macro, select **Tools | Macro | Macros**. Select the macro, then click **Delete**. Select **Yes** at the prompt and **Close**.*

9. Save the presentation and leave it open.

10. Select **Tools | Customize**.

11. From the **Commands** tab, scroll down the **Categories** list and select **New Menu**.

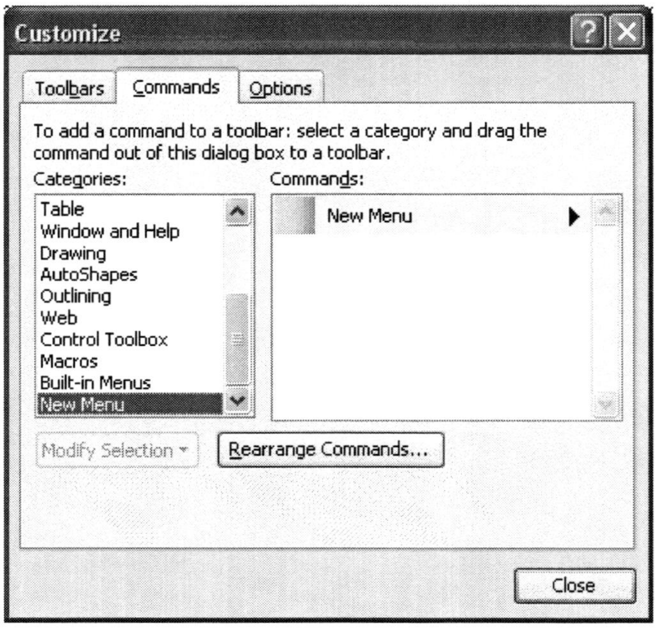

12. The **New Menu** is shown at the right of the dialog box, click on it and hold down the mouse button.

13. Drag the command to the **Menu Bar** in between the **Edit** and **View** menu as shown, 

, and release.

14. Scroll down the **Categories** list and select **Macros**.

15. Click and drag the command **Handouts** up to the **New Menu,** a small drop down box appears, 

, release the mouse button and the command drops on to the menu.

16. Click and drag the **SavePrint** command up to the **New Menu** in the same way.

17. Click on the text, **New Menu,** click **Modify Selection** in the dialog box and in **Name**, delete the text **New Menu** and type in **Custom,** 

.

18. Close the **Customize** dialog box and save the presentation.

> ***Note:*** *One way to provide evidence of a macro is to obtain a screen print of the programming code behind it.*

19. Select **Tools | Macro | Macros**, select the **SavePrint** macro, click **Edit**, the **Microsoft Visual Basic** window is displayed. This shows the Visual Basic code behind the macro. It is not required to understand the code at this level.

20. Create a screen print of the **Microsoft Visual Basic** window.

21. Select **File | Close and Return to Microsoft PowerPoint**.

22. Open the **Evidence** document and paste the screen print.

23. In **Normal View**, create a screen print showing the **Custom Menu** and **Print Handouts** button on the **Standard Toolbar**.

24. Paste this into the **Evidence** document and enter suitable captions below the images. Save and close the document.

25. Delete the **Print Handouts** button, **Custom** menu and all macros from **Macro** (see the note on the previous page).

26. Delete the **Handouts** macro from the **Macro** presentation.

27. Close the presentation, saving the changes if prompted.

> ***Note:*** *If **Macro Security** is set to **Medium**, when opening a file containing macros a warning message will appear. There are 3 options available: **Disable Macros, Enable Macros, More Info**. Select **Enable Macros**. This will allow the macros to be run when the file is open.*

Exercise 53 - Develop Your Skills

1. Open the presentation **High Close** in **Slide Sorter View**.

2. You have decided to record a macro to print the custom show **Brief** to save preparation time, prior to the show. Select slide **1**, select **Tools | Macro | Record New Macro.** Name the macro **Custom**.

3. Select **File | Print**, select **Custom Show** from the **Print range** and then select **Brief**. Click **OK** and stop recording.

4. As you cannot decide whether to include a footer on every slide, you are going to record a macro to insert a footer on one slide only. Select slide **2**, select **Tools | Macro | Record New Macro.** Name the macro **Footer**.

5. Select **View | Header and Footer**. Select **Update automatically** and check **Slide number**. In the **Footer** enter **Your Name**. Click **Apply** and stop recording.

6. Run the macro **Footer** for slide **3.** You have decided to include a footer on every slide in your presentation.

7. Assign the macro **Footer** to a button on the toolbar. Run the macro for every slide apart from slide **1**.

8. The Vice-Principal has sent you a memo asking you to include the title of **College of Excellence** in the presentation. You are going to record a macro to insert the text in the footer area of the slide and to print that slide. Move to slide **7**. Select **Tools | Macro | Record New Macro.** Name the macro **Text**.

9. Select **View | Header and Footer**. In the **Footer** box delete the existing text and type **College of Excellence**. Click **Apply**.

10. Select **File | Print**, **Current Slide**. Click **OK** and stop recording.

11. Save the presentation.

12. You are going to record a macro to save the presentation as a **PowerPoint Show**.

> ***Note:*** *If you open a presentation saved as a PowerPoint Show from* ***Folders View****, it automatically starts as a slide show.*

13. Select **Tools | Macro | Record New Macro**. Name the macro **Show**.

14. Select **File | Save As**, from the **Save as type** drop down list, select **PowerPoint Show(*.pps)**. Change the file name to **High Close2** and click **Save**. Stop recording.

15. Close the presentation **High Close2**.

16. Open the presentation **High Close**. Select **Enable Macros**.

17. In **Normal View**, select **Tools | Customize** and the **Macros** command. Drag the command **Custom** to the **Standard Toolbar**. Rename the button **Print Custom**.

18. Select **Tools | Customize** and the **New Menu** command. Drag the command up to the **Menu Bar**. Rename the new menu **Personal**.

19. Drag the macro **Text** up to the **Personal** menu.

20. Close the **Customize** dialog box.

21. Create screen prints of all the recorded macros and paste into the **Revision Evidence** document.

22. Create a screen print showing the **Personal Menu** and **Print Custom** button. Paste into the **Revision Evidence** document. Enter suitable captions below the images.

23. Save and close the document and close *Word*.

24. Remove the **Personal** menu and **Print Custom** button from the **Menu Bar** and toolbar.

25. Save the presentation and close it.

Summary: Macros

Your ITQ evidence must demonstrate the following skills:

- Format technically complex and interactive presentations using appropriate tools and techniques.

Read through the exercises in this Skill Set to give you some ideas of how you could demonstrate these skills.

Skill Set 7

Finishing and Printing

By the end of this Skill Set you should be able to:

Add Speaker's Notes
Create Start and End Slides
Create a Summary Slide
Check a Presentation
Review, Compare and Merge Presentations
Print Slides and Presentations in Different Formats
Use Package for CD
Publish to the Web

Exercise 54 - Adding Speaker's Notes

Notes can be added to any or all slides in a presentation. The notes can be to prompt the speaker as he or she runs the slide show, or for the benefit of the audience, as they can be printed and handed out. If they are to be used as a prompt for the presenter, the notes should be in a larger font than normal, so that they can be read easily.

Activity:

1. Open the **Progressive Training** presentation and close the **Task Pane**.

2. Select slide **12** and select **View | Notes Page**. The example below is shown viewed at **52%**.

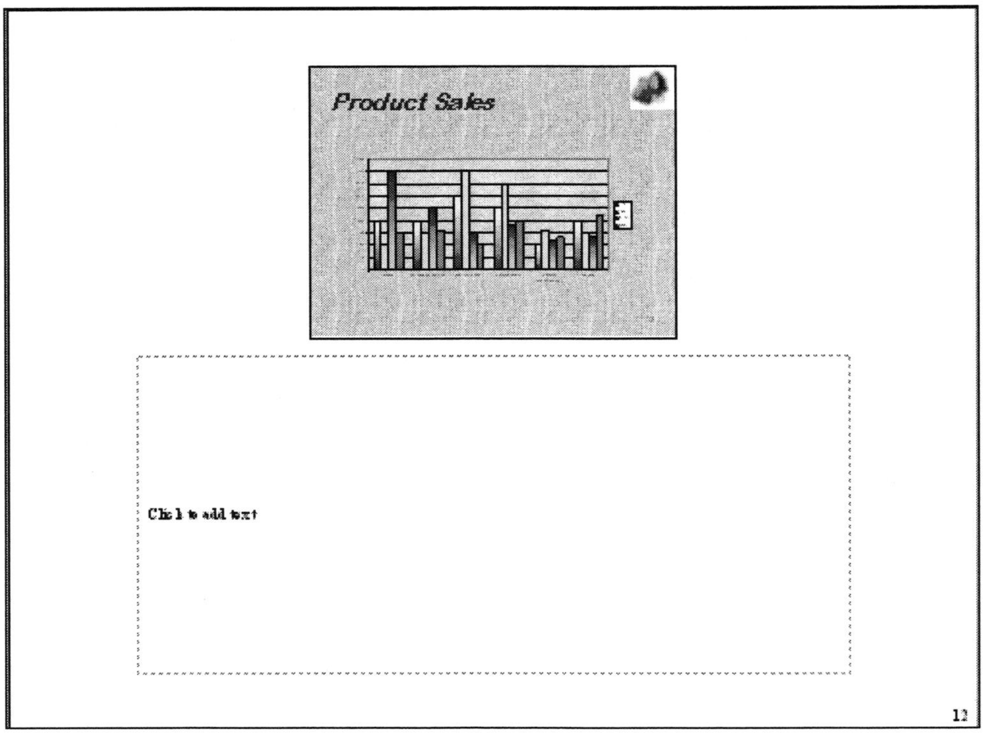

3. Click in the white area beneath the slide and zoom in to **100%**.

4. Type in the following note for the speaker:

   Our Sales are below average for April. Press <**Enter**>.

   We will have to consider offering a discount on our products from May to try and boost our sales.

5. Switch to **Slide Sorter View**.

6. Save the presentation and leave it open.

Exercise 55 - Start and End Slides

As well as the main slides in a presentation which show the required content, it is good practice to include slides which help to define the overall structure of the presentation. The start is almost always defined by using a **Title Slide**, as you have done in the current presentation. This usually defines the subject matter that the presentation will follow and will typically display the name of a company or product or project.

Sometimes a blank slide is used to indicate the end of a presentation. This can be particularly useful for a speaker presenting the show, as it gives an opportunity for them to make closing remarks, etc. after all the content slides have been shown, but while the presentation is still on the screen.

Summary slides, which are covered in the next exercise, can be created to act like content pages for the slides that follow them.

Activity:

1. Open the **Progressive Training** presentation if not open already from the previous exercise.

2. In **Slide Sorter View**, select the last slide, slide **12**.

3. Insert a new slide, choosing the **Blank** slide layout.

4. Notice that the graphic and background effect are applied to this slide, as they were added in **Slide Master View**.

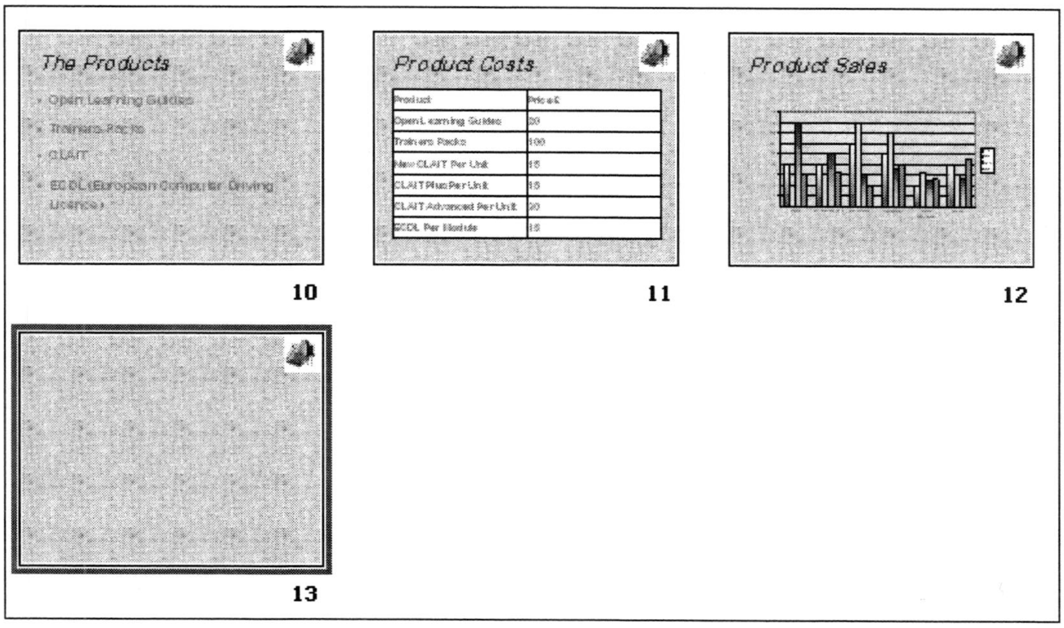

5. Save the presentation and leave it open.

Exercise 56 - Creating a Summary Slide

At certain points of your presentation you may want to summarise some main points on a **Summary Slide**. A **Summary Slide** can be automatically created by selecting the titles of the required slides, which become bulleted items on the **Summary Slide**.

If a **Summary Slide** is created for all of the slides in a presentation and placed as the first slide, it can be used as an **Agenda** or **Contents** slide. A summary slide does not affect the layout of any other slide in the presentation.

Activity:

1. Open the **Progressive Training** presentation, if not open already from the previous exercise.

2. In **Slide Sorter** view, select slide **3**, then hold down the <**Ctrl**> key and select slides **6**, **8** and **10**.

3. Click the **Summary Slide** button, . The slide is created and inserted after slide **2**. The **Summary Slide** becomes slide **3 of 14**.

4. Double click on the new slide to view it in **Normal View**.

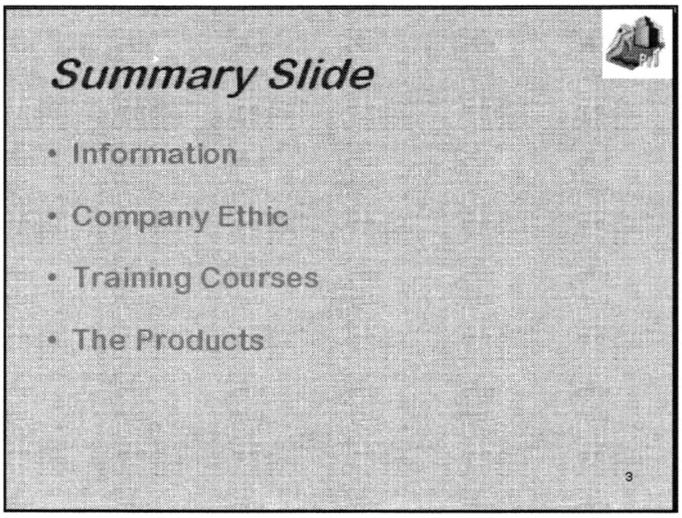

5. Notice how the text in the bulleted list consists of the titles of the four selected slides. Once created, the slide is like any other and can be edited. Change the title on the slide to **In Summary**.

6. Switch to **Slide Sorter** view.

7. Move the **Summary Slide** so that it will appear just before the final blank slide when the presentation is run.

8. Save the **Progressive Training** presentation and close it.

Exercise 57 - Perfecting Your Presentation

Having spent considerable time in designing your presentation it is important that it is produced to a professional standard. Your presentation should be checked very carefully for spelling mistakes. All the documentation, which you provide as evidence, should be checked thoroughly and presented in a professional manner.

Activity:

1. Open the presentation **Spelling**. Any spelling errors are underlined in red.

2. In **Normal View**, view slide **1**. Click the **Spelling** button, , on the **Standard Toolbar**. The **Spelling** dialog box is displayed.

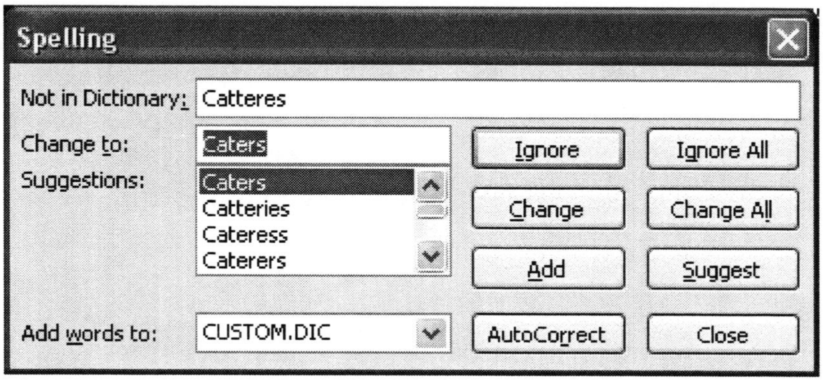

3. The first spelling error **Catteres** is selected on slide **2**. From the **Suggestions** list, select **Catteries** and click **Change**.

4. The next spelling error, **volunter**, is selected. From the list, select **volunteer** and click **Change**. Continue working through the presentation making the corrections. The following message appears when the check is complete.

5. Click **OK**.

6. Close the presentation <u>without</u> saving.

Note: *You can check your spelling as you type.*

7. Open the **Spelling** presentation again.

8. In **Normal View**, move to slide **2**, right click on the word **Catteres**, which is underlined in red. A shortcut menu appears.

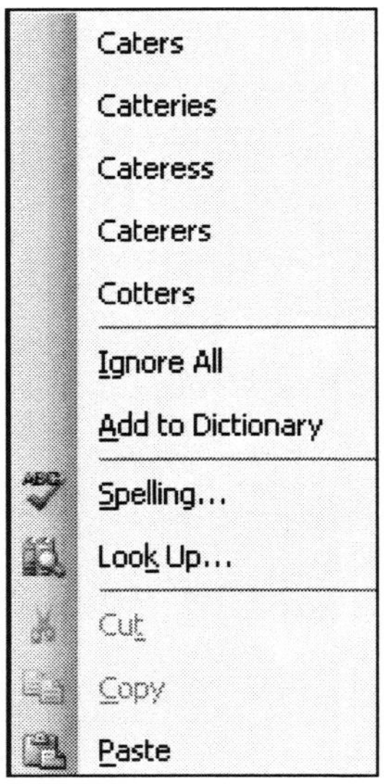

9. Select the word **Catteries** and the error is corrected.

10. Continue working through the presentation correcting all spelling errors using the shortcut menu.

11. Save the presentation as **Cattery**.

Note: *A note of caution: automatic spell checkers only highlight words they do not recognise. They will not highlight incorrectly used words, such as* ***horse*** *instead of* ***hoarse*** *or spelling mistakes where the result is still a valid word, such as* ***her*** *instead of* ***here****. It is always a good idea to manually check a document to identify any such errors.*

12. A presentation that is considered complete can be saved in a format that by default will always open as a slide show. Select **File | Save As** and save the presentation as **Cattery**, in the data file folder, but change the **Save as type** setting to **PowerPoint Show (*.pps)**.

13. Close the presentation and close *PowerPoint*.

14. In **Folders View**, locate and open the supplied data folder.

15. Double click **Cattery.pps** to open it. The presentation will open as a slide show. Run through the show to the end. At the end of the show **Folders View** will be redisplayed.

Note: *The PowerPoint application is still required for a* ***PowerPoint Show*** *to be viewed.*

16. Close the window.

Exercise 58 - Reviewing

A method of receiving feedback on presentations under development is to use the **reviewing** process. Versions of a presentation are sent to reviewers over a network or via e-mail. Reviewers can make their suggested changes and return the files. The suggested changes can be evaluated and incorporated into the original presentation if required.

Activity:

1. Start *PowerPoint* and open the **Retreat** presentation. Save it immediately as **Original**. As the author of the presentation **Original**, you will be sending a copy of this out for review.

2. One way to send out the file is via e-mail. To do this, select **File | Send to | Mail Recipient (for Review)**. Your mail messaging application will start with all the necessary information entered, except the address.

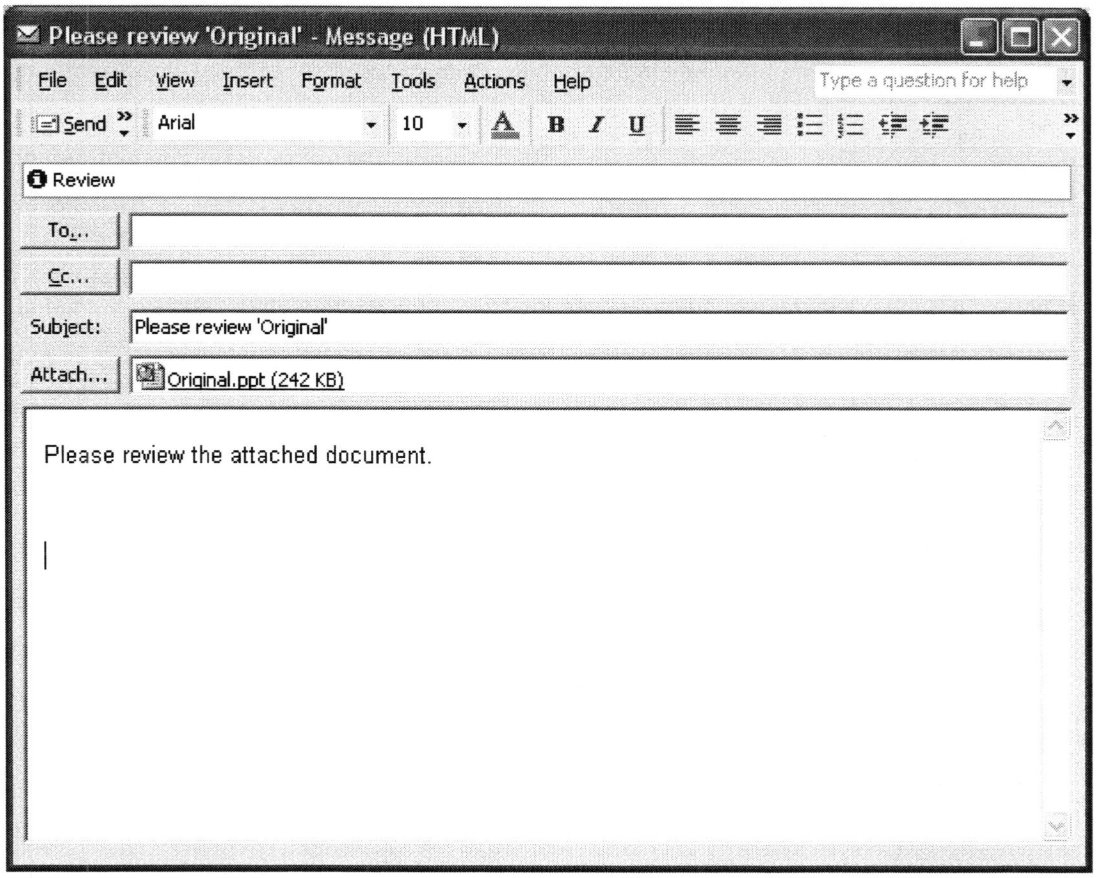

3. You will not use this method here however, so that the exercise may be completed without Internet access. Close the message window <u>without</u> sending or saving.

4. To send the file to someone locally, select **File | Save As**.

5. Make sure **Save in** shows the location of the supplied data files, and change the file name to **Version1**.

6. Click the drop down arrow for **Save as type** and select **Presentation for Review (*.ppt)**.

7. Click **Save** then close the presentation.

8. Open the **Version1** presentation as the reviewer. If there is a message about merging changes, click **No**.

9. Suggested amendments can now be made to the presentation. Highlight the title **Serenity Lodge** on slide **1** and make it italic.

10. On slide **4 Physical**, add a new bullet point **Sonic Therapy Lounge**.

11. On slide **6**, insert a **Clip Art** image using the search **dove**.

12. Move it to the bottom right corner of the slide and reduce its size by about half.

13. Save the presentation and close it.

Exercise 59 - Compare and Merge

When copies of a presentation have been sent for review and have been amended, the author can compare them directly with the original and either accept or reject the suggestions.

Activity:

1. Open the **Original** presentation as the author. You are going to review the proposed amendments. Make sure **Normal View** is displayed.

2. Select **Tools | Compare and Merge Presentations**. Locate the **Version1** file, select it and click **Merge**.

Note: *More than one file could be selected for merging if for example a Version2 had been created and had been amended by another user.*

3. The **Reviewing** toolbar and a **Revisions Task Pane** will be displayed. The **Revisions** pane has two tabs. Click the **List** tab to see a list of all amendments for the current slide. Click the **Gallery** tab to see a picture of the amended slide. Make sure **List** is selected. Paste a screen print in to the **Evidence** document and annotate it appropriately.

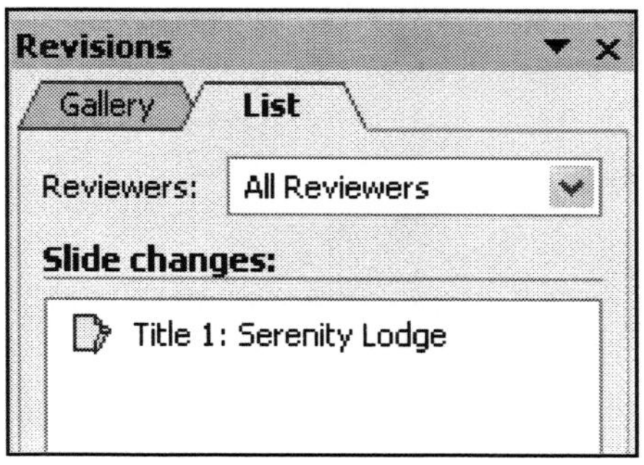

4. The first slide has suggested amendments, and this is indicated by an icon, , in the appropriate place on the slide, and by an entry in the task pane.

Note: *The icons are colour coded to distinguish amendments from different reviewers.*

5. Click either the entry or the icon to expand the amendment action and the name of the reviewer.

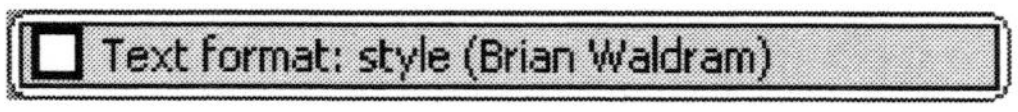

6. Click the box at the left of the action to accept it and change the original presentation. The icon on the slide shows a tick to indicate an accepted amendment. Paste an example of an accepted amendment into **Evidence**.

7. Click the **Next Item** button, , on the **Reviewing** toolbar to open the next amendment.

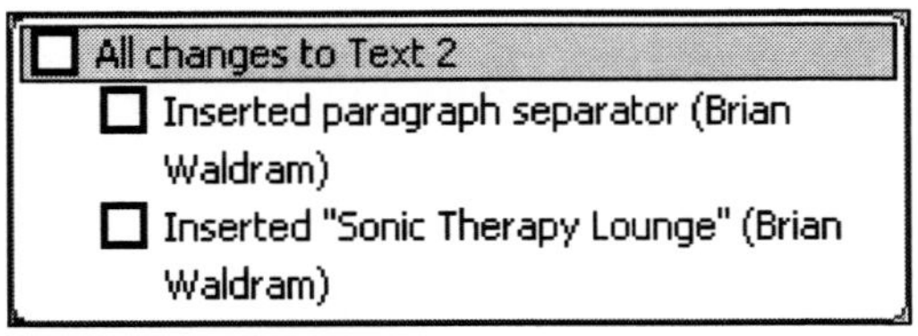

8. Notice this amendment consists of two actions. Either action could be accepted separately, but in this exercise click the box on the top line to accept both of them.

9. Click  to move to the next amendments, on slide **6**. This time click the **Gallery** tab.

10. Click the slide image in the task pane to apply all changes (from this reviewer) to this slide.

11. Click  to move to the next amendment. The inserted image is already shown as amended, because the **Gallery** tab was used.

12. Click . This is the end of the presentation. Click **Cancel**.

13. Select slide **1** again. You decide that you don't like the italic title. Click the amendment icon on the slide to display the details and then click on the details to remove the check and discard (un-apply) the changes.

> ***Note:*** *Clicking the slide image in the task pane would also remove all changes from this slide.* ***Apply*** *and* ***Unapply*** *buttons are also available on the* ***Review*** *toolbar.*

14. Save the **Original** presentation and close it.

15. Re-open the **Original** presentation. It is still in review mode and the **Version1** amendments can still be seen in the **Revisions** task pane. Further applying or removing of changes can still be performed.

16. Click the **End Review** button on the **Reviewing** toolbar.

17. Read the warning message and click **Yes**. The review cycle is now ended. If further reviewing is required, the whole cycle must be restarted by sending out this version for review again.

18. Save the **Original** presentation and close it.

Exercise 60 - Printing Slides and Presentations

Various aspects of a presentation may be printed out, such as slide images, handouts, speaker notes and slide content. You can print slides in various formats, as well as screen prints from the design process as evidence of certain features.

Activity:

1. Open the **Progressive Training** presentation and select **File | Page Setup**.

2. Make sure the orientation for **Slides** is set to **Landscape** and the orientation for all **Notes, handouts & outline** is set to **Portrait**.

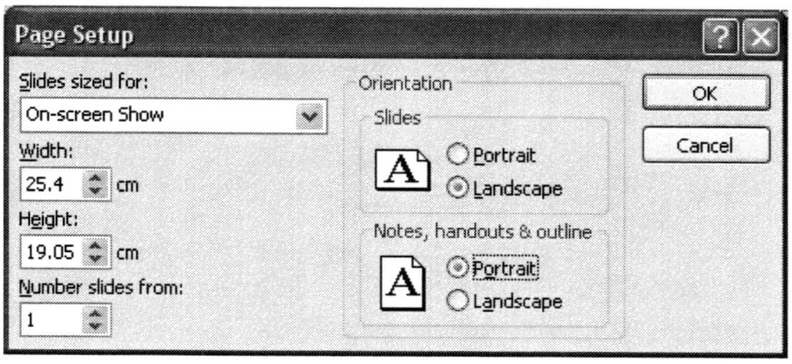

3. Click **OK** then click the **Print** button, , on the toolbar. One copy of every slide in the presentation will be printed on the default printer, assuming there is one connected.

4. In **Slide Sorter View**, select the third slide and select **File | Print**. The **Print** dialog box appears.

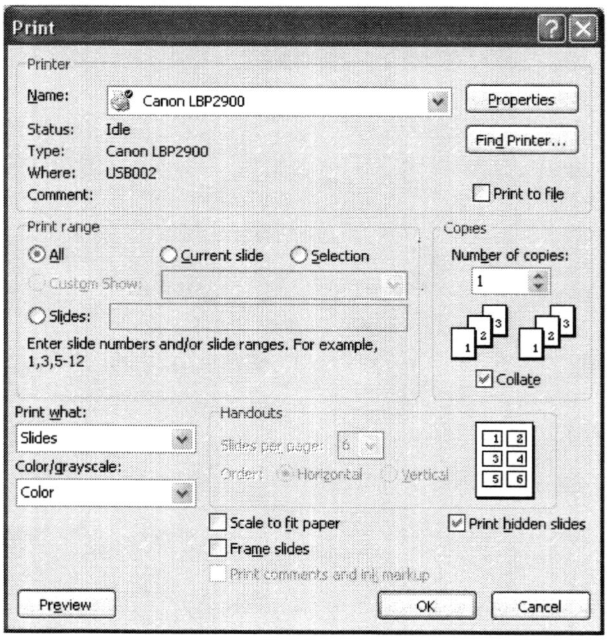

5. Make sure that **Slides** is selected under **Print what** and unless you have a colour printer and particularly want to see the colour effects, select **Grayscale** as the **Color/grayscale** setting.

6. From **Print range**, choose **Current slide**. Set **Number of copies** to **2**, then click **OK** to print **2** copies of slide **3** only.

7. Handouts, in the form of several miniature slides printed on one sheet, can be printed for an audience to follow as the presentation is running. They can also use them for reference and as a reminder of the presentation. Select **File | Print** again.

8. From **Print range**, choose **Slides** and type **1-3** and from the **Print what** drop down list, select **Handouts**.

9. Drop down the list next to **Slides per page** and select **3**. The small preview at the right of this section shows how the printout will appear. **Grayscale** is already selected in the **Color/grayscale** box. Leave this option selected, but be aware that it will need changing should colour prints be required.

Note: *Selecting 3 slides per page prints a small slide image (thumbnail) and an area for user notes for each slide.*

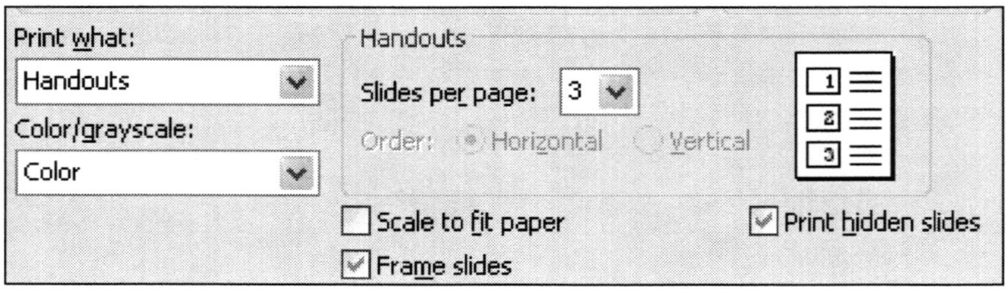

10. Click **OK** to print handouts.

11. A presentation can be printed in **Notes Page** view, i.e. a slide image with any added notes underneath. This could be useful as a script for the presenter during the public showing of the presentation. Select **File | Print**.

12. Select **12** in the **Slides** box in **Print range**.

Note: *Slide **12** had notes added in Exercise **54**.*

13. From **Print what** select **Notes Pages** and click **OK**. The slide image is printed with any speaker notes underneath.

14. Close the presentation without saving the changes.

Exercise 61 - Package for CD

A presentation can be "packaged" to be used on a different computer. The **Package for CD** feature keeps all of the relevant files and fonts in the same location, and supplies a **PowerPoint Viewer** so the presentation can be viewed on any computer, even if *PowerPoint* is not installed.

Activity:

1. Open the **Holidays2** presentation.

> **Note:** *In PowerPoint 2003* ***Pack and Go*** *(compressing to a floppy disk) has been replaced by* ***Package for CD****, which allows the presentation and viewer to be copied to CD. This means that you must have a CD writer on your computer. If you only have a floppy disk drive, insert a blank disk into the drive and at step 3 uncheck* ***PowerPoint Viewer****, as the viewer is too big for a floppy disk.*

2. Select **File | Package for CD**. In the **Name the CD** box enter **Holiday**.

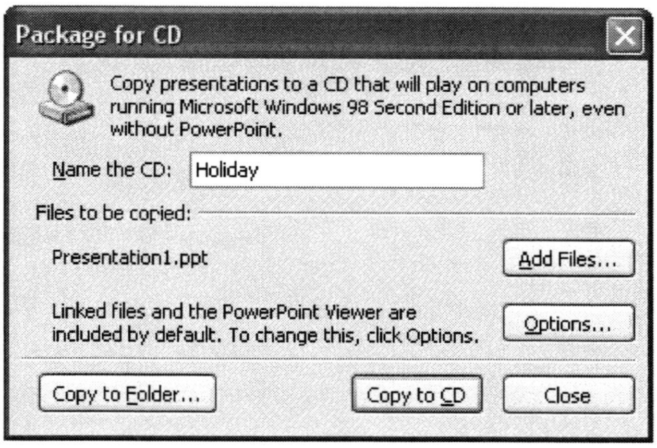

3. Click **Options**. Ensure the following options are checked.

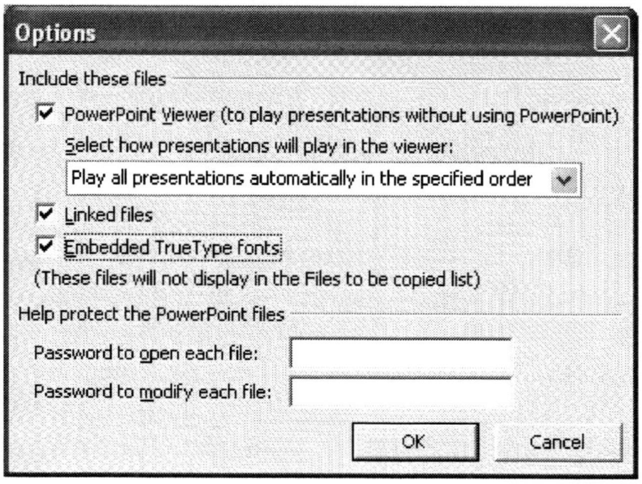

Note: *If you are using a floppy disk you cannot add the **Viewer**. Do not check the **PowerPoint Viewer** option. This means you can only show the presentation on a computer with PowerPoint installed.*

4. Click **OK**. Now click the **Copy to Folder** button.

Note: *For the purposes of this exercise, copy the files to the data folder on the hard drive of the computer. In practice, if you are copying to a CD, click **Copy to CD**, then follow the instructions.*

5. Click **Browse**. From **Look in**, select the location of the data files.

Note: *If you are copying to a floppy disk, without the **Viewer**, select the floppy disk drive from **Look in**.*

6. Click **Select** and then **OK**.

7. The files are copied to the data folder. Click **Close**.

8. Close the presentation. Make sure that *PowerPoint* is not running.

9. In **Folders View**, click on the folder icon of the data folder in the navigation pane.

10. Double click the **Holiday** folder. All of the files necessary to run the presentation are displayed in the folder. Ensure **Details** view is selected.

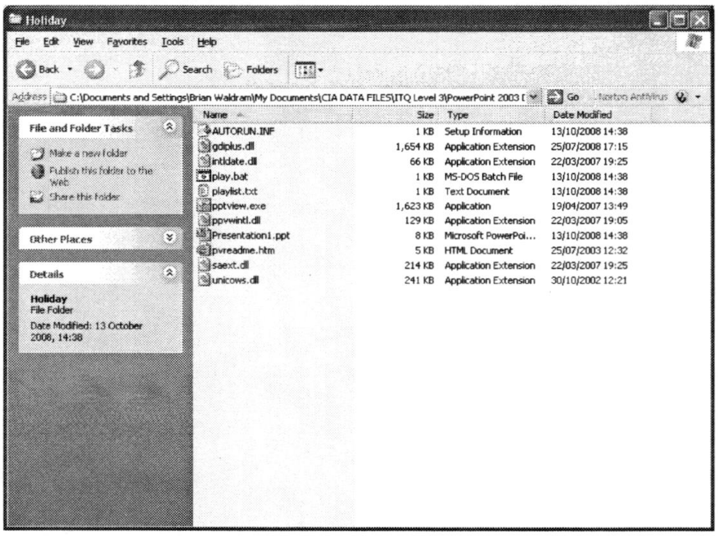

11. Double click pptview.exe (this is what you would click if you had copied to a CD, then put the CD into another computer). If this is the first time the viewer has been used, you'll need to accept the licence.

12. Double click the **Holidays2** icon in the viewer to start the show.

13. Click to advance the show, then close the viewer when finished.

14. Close any open windows.

Exercise 62 - Publishing to the Web

A finished presentation can be published to the Web, if desired. It is a good idea to preview the presentation in a web browser before publishing it. The presentation must be saved as a web page before being published.

> **Note:** *The user must have an Internet connection and service provider before any web pages can be published to the Internet. A completed web site is either published to an Internet Service Provider or a server machine within your organisation (this is called an Intranet - a network set up by an organisation, to enable all colleagues to access web pages from all computers on the network). If necessary, ask the IT Administrator which connection is available before completing this section.*

Activity:

1. Open the **Training** presentation (saved in **Exercise 12**).

2. In **Normal View**, select **File | Save as Web Page**. Change the **File name** to **Training Promotion** and select a saving location from the **Save in** drop down list or **Folder** list.

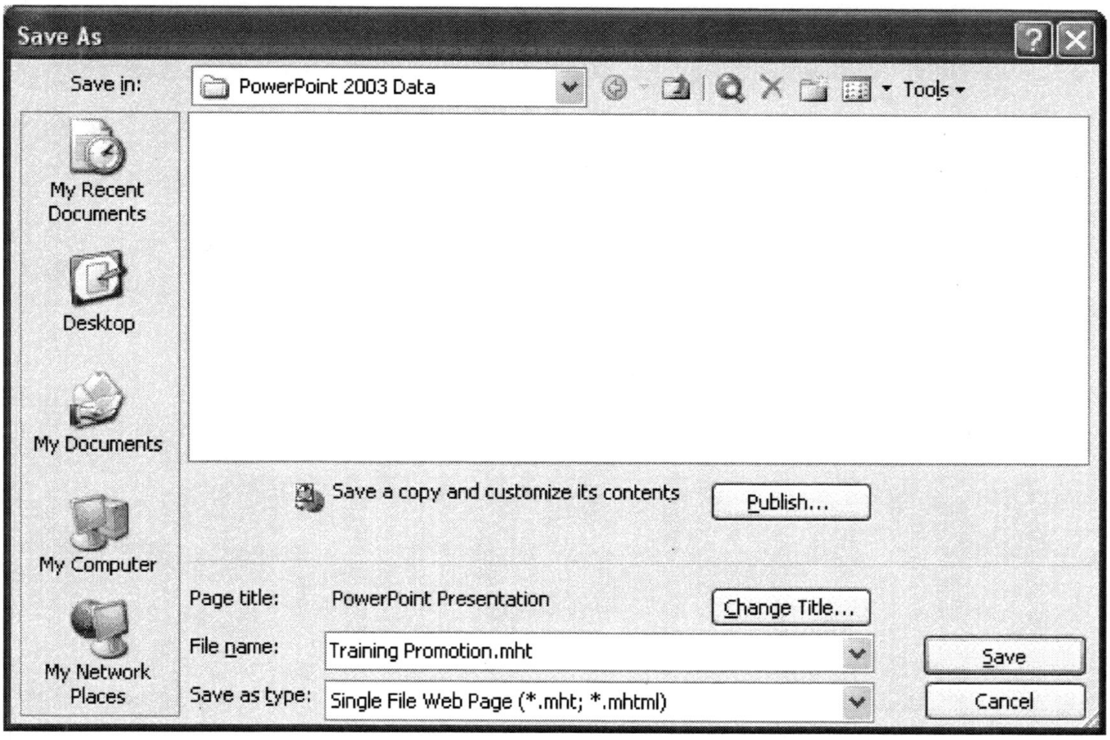

3. Click the **Publish** button.

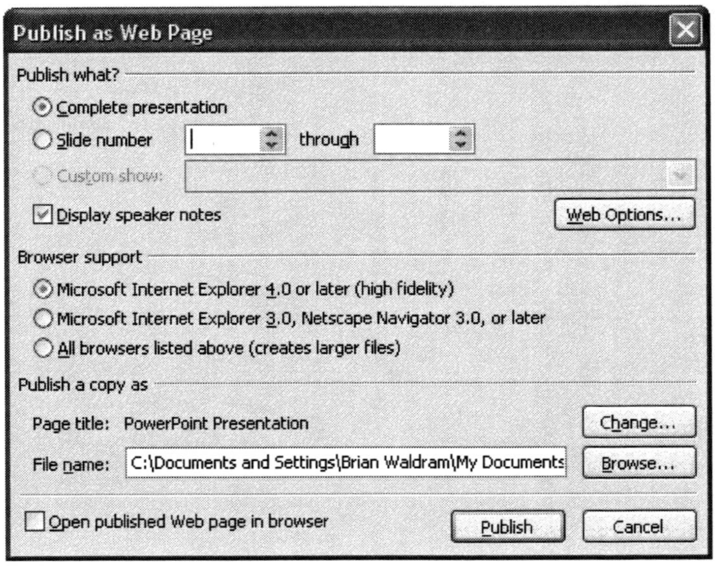

> ***Note:*** *If you do not want speaker notes to appear on the web page, uncheck the box,* ***Display speaker notes****.*

4. In the **Publish what?** area leave the default setting as **Complete presentation** (single slides or a number of slides can be published as a web page*)*. Select the correct options for **Browser support** and place a check in **Open published Web page in browser**.

5. Click **Publish** to publish the presentation as a web page.

> ***Note:*** *When the browser opens, there may be a message about Internet Explorer versions. Click the prompt* ***here*** *to continue.*

6. There may be a security message banner when the browser opens. Click on it and select **Allow Blocked Content**. Click **Yes** at the dialog box.

7. The screen is divided into two sections. The slide titles appear at the left of the screen on the **Outline** navigating bar. Move the selection pointer over title **2,** the selection pointer changes to a hyperlink and the text colour changes to yellow. Click to move to slide **2**.

> ***Note:*** *You should produce evidence of the presentation published as a Web Page.*

8. Create a screen print of the browser screen, showing the **Outline** navigating bar. Paste this into your the **Evidence** document with a suitable caption.

9. Save and close the document. Close *Word.*

10. Close the browser window using the **Close** button, ☒.

11. Save and close the **Training** presentation.

Exercise 63 - Develop Your Skills

1. Open the presentation **High Close** in **Notes Page View**.

2. You want to make a note of the college aims for next year, in case you forget to mention them in your presentation. Move to slide **6**, **Retention Rates**. Add the notes:

   The retention rates over the last 5 years have steadily improved.
   Aims
   Achieve a 95% retention rate by next year.
   New initiatives to attract more adult learners.
   Identify ways in which adults can be directed to a more positive approach to learning.

3. Change to **Slide Sorter View**. Insert a final **Blank** slide.

4. Create a **Summary** slide, after slide **7**, to summarise slides **8**, **13**, **14**, **16** and **19**.

5. Add the speaker's note **Mention these points in brief**, to the new slide.

6. Move the **Summary** slide to appear before the slide **All Systems Go**.

7. Check your presentation carefully correcting any spelling errors.

8. Save the presentation. It is now to be saved so that it can be run on another computer.

9. Select **File | Package for CD** and follow the instructions carefully.

10. The Vice-Principal would like the finished presentation published on the World Wide Web. Open the **High Close** presentation (*not the compressed presentation)* if not already open.

11. In **Normal View**, select **File | Save as Web Page**. Change the file name to **High Close FE College**. Publish the complete presentation. Remember you may have to **Allow Blocked Content**.

12. Create a screen print of the presentation shown in a browser screen. Paste into the **Revision Evidence** document with a suitable caption.

13. Save the document and close *Word*.

14. Print the presentation slides.

15. Print the presentation in handout format, 6 to a page.

16. Print the presentation showing speaker's notes.

17. Close the presentation and *PowerPoint*.

Summary: Finishing and Printing

Your ITQ evidence must demonstrate the following skills:

- Convert files to another format where necessary
- Use advanced techniques for combining or merging versions of information from different users
- Check that structure, style and formatting are used to communicate effectively
- Save presentation slides as a standalone show and as web pages.

You need to know and understand

- How to produce information that communicates effectively, by structuring the content to take account of different contexts and audience needs.

Read through the exercises in this Skill Set to give you some ideas of how you could demonstrate these skills.

Evidence Requirements

You will need to produce at least **three substantial and complex** tasks for your assessor to judge and decide whether you have met the requirements of this unit. These tasks may:

- be fully supported by evidence which has come from your job in the workplace. This evidence may contribute towards the mandatory unit - Make selective use of IT.
- come from simulation. This evidence **will not** be able to be used for the mandatory unit.

These tasks must show that you have done and know everything from the Level 3 Checklist.

Planning

For each task, you must show that you have designed a document that is appropriate for that specific task and aimed at a specific audience. You will need to make design notes about the content of the document and list reasons why you have chosen the format, e.g. report, memo, brochure. You must demonstrate your understanding of what makes a document communicate information effectively.

When planning your chosen task, some thought should be given to how you are going to obtain the desired result. The planning should include the content and explain where that content fits into the finished resource. Think about who it's for, how they would like the information to be presented and how it is to be used. Plan the content in detail and address how the task is to be completed. Before starting, refer to the evidence checklist to make sure that your completed task will include all the required elements.

Design Notes

Design notes should be kept throughout the planning process. Changes to the specification, feedback from users, comments and decisions taken should all be logged. These design notes should be included in your final submission. They can be in the form of a *Word* document, or a flowchart or storyboard.

Suggestions for Comprehensive Tasks

These suggested tasks are to help you develop your own ideas, which should be relevant to your own workplace (or workplace simulation). You could produce something similar to the suggestions below. *Please note that each task may not cover all evidence required for the unit in its own right.* Make sure that you obtain printouts and screen shots as you are creating your own documents, so that they can be used as ITQ evidence.

- The presentations used in the course of this guide could all be adapted to be suitable types of task for this unit. Examine them to see if you could use the ideas within them to create your own solutions. It is essential that these examples are only used to show the sort of tasks that could be used. They must not be submitted in their own right.

- Create a presentation about your company/organisation to be used as part of a team building day. Add a corporate logo to the master slide and format using the company colours. Include video and audio clips and animation (you could import an existing video clip into *Windows Movie Maker* and try some editing). Alternatively, import digital images into the presentation and apply animation and sound effects to them.

- Create a continuously running presentation which promotes and explains a company product. This could highlight key benefits of the product, describe how the product works, suggest when and where it could be used, and display details of the costing structure including any introductory offers. Import information from other software, e.g. spreadsheets or word processing documents. Include sound and animation to make the presentation interesting. Send the draft presentation to a colleague for review. Incorporate their suggestions in the completed version.

- Create an induction presentation for new starters to your company/organisation. This could include slides describing various departments, pictures of key staff, and details of pension schemes, social clubs, etc. It could also be a place to display some of the key conditions of employment and any rules and instructions peculiar to your company/organisation. It would be useful for such a presentation to have a comprehensive system of hyperlinks and bookmarks so that users can easily access the areas that interest them. Package the file to a CD, or save it as a *PowerPoint* show, so that it can be run on any computer.

- Create a presentation to summarise a training or teaching course that you are running. Include the aims and key features of the course, and details of the individual topics covered. Other items which could be put into the presentation include background information, which could be displayed only where required and a list of potential discussion points. By including comprehensive speaker's notes, the presentation could be printed out as handouts and used as a useful set of notes to accompany the course. Save the presentation in a format that could be viewed on the web.

Presentation Software Level 3 Checklist

WHAT YOU NEED TO DO		
1	Convert files to another suitable format, where necessary.	☐
2	Export and import, link objects between different software.	☐
3	Make references to external data. • For example: hyperlinks, object linking and embedding.	☐
4	Use advanced techniques for combining or merging versions of information from different users.	☐
5	Use a wide range of editing techniques to produce technically complex and interactive presentations. • For example: cutting, rendering and exporting video clips; digitising and cutting sound clips from a microphone.	☐
6	Check sound and moving images are edited appropriately.	☐
7	Check that structure, style and formatting are used to communicate effectively.	☐
8	Rehearse and check timing of a slide show.	☐
9	Format technically complex and interactive presentations using appropriate tools and techniques. • For example: creating a master slide to format consistently; using different formats in each section and creating different slide transitions.	☐
10	Create interactive slides using time-line based tools.	☐
11	Create new scenes using video editing software.	☐
12	Play sound through a computer as part of a presentation.	☐
13	Save presentation slides as a standalone show and as web pages.	☐
WHAT YOU NEED TO KNOW AND UNDERSTAND		
A	How to produce information that communicates effectively, by structuring the content to take account of different contexts and audience needs.	☐
B	How to produce technically complex and interactive presentations. Technically complex and interactive presentations need to be produced using time-line based tools and may include sound and moving images.	☐
C	How to include digitised sound and moving images, such as by recording sound through a computer, digitising sound from a microphone and capturing video.	☐
D	What sound and image formats are suitable.	☐

Glossary

Action Button A button placed on a slide that can have actions attached such as: navigating to another slide, or presentation, opening another application or playing a sound clip.

AutoShapes Ready-made shapes in a variety of categories, which are available from a menu on the **Drawing** toolbar.

Chart Effects Custom animations specific to elements within a chart.

Clip Art A store of graphic images that is available within all *Office* applications.

Colour Scheme A set of pre-defined colours applied to specific areas of a slide.

Custom Animation Allows the appearance, movement and sound effects attached to any slide object to be specified and customised.

Custom Show A subset of slides within a show that can be created to be relevant to a specific target audience.

Design Template A pre-set design, including colours and fonts that can be applied to slides.

Drawing Objects Objects that can be created directly on the slide using tools on the **Drawing** toolbar.

Embedded Object An object on a slide is described as embedded if it is not linked to a source file.

Flowchart A diagram using **AutoShapes** to illustrate systems, processes or procedures.

Hyperlink A link attached to a selected object or piece of text that when clicked in **Slide Show** view, navigates to: another location within the same slide, a different slide, a different presentation or application. Hyperlinks can also be attached to e-mail or web site addresses.

Linking Data from external sources, e.g. text, data, charts etc. can be linked (different from hyperlinking) to *PowerPoint* slides, so that any changes to the source data is automatically applied to the object on the slide.

Macro A sequence of actions or commands, which is recorded and saved to be re-used.

Organisation Chart A diagram displaying the hierarchical staffing structure of an organisation.

Package for CD	A feature that stores all slides and objects within a presentation and copies them to CD, ready for distribution.
Position	A setting available within the **Format** dialog box for any object that allows its precise position to be specified as a pair of measurements from either the top left or centre of the slide.
Review	Send a presentation to others for comments.
Save as an Image	An entire presentation, or the currently selected slide within a presentation, can be saved as a graphic image to be used as an object within other applications.
Slide Layout	The type of slide specified; e.g. **Title and Text**, Title **Only**, etc.
Slide Master	A view that is used to specify settings/formatting and/or add objects that will appear on every slide except the **Title Master**.
Slide Show	A presentation being run on screen, with all effects, transitions, sounds, etc.
Style Sheet	A document giving specific details of all text styles, spacing and formatting used within a presentation.
Summary Slide	A slide created automatically from a number of selected slides. The titles from the selected slides are displayed as bulleted items on the resulting slide.
Template	A presentation framework containing formatting, saved so that it can be used as the basis for future presentations.
Text Box	A frame that can be drawn on the background of a slide, into which text may be typed. Text cannot be typed directly onto a slide.
Title Master	A view that is used to specify settings/formatting and/or add objects, which will appear on every slide based on the **Title Slide** layout.
Transitions	Special effects that occur as one slide changes to the next during a slide show. Timings and sound effects may be specified as well as visual effects.
Views	Different ways of looking at the slides within a presentation.
WordArt	A special text feature that may be inserted on to a slide as a drawing object.

Index

Action Buttons 83

Editing 86

Animation

Clips 37

Charts 72

Introducing 69

Sequences 70

Background

Effects 20

Object 32

Bullet

Levels 14

Charts

Formatting 46, 51

Importing 50, 51

Inserting 50

Organisation 44

Clip Art

Inserting 36

Colour Schemes 18

Compare and Merge 119

Custom Shows 80

Running 82

Design Considerations 10

Drawn Objects 31

Editing Video 67

Evidence

Producing 26

Formatting

Chart 46, 51

Handouts

Printing 122

Hide

Slides 79

Hyperlinks 87

Import

Chart 50, 53

Insert

Animated Clips 37

Chart 50

Clip Art 36

Movies 65

Organisation Chart 44

Picture 38

Slides 77

Sounds 63

Table 48

WordArt 34

Line Spacing 15

Linking 54

Modifying Linked Data 56

Macros

Assigning 105

Multiple Action 104

Recording 102

Running 103

Master

Notes Page 17

Slide 12

Title 16

Movies

Editing 67

File Types 67

Inserting 65

Notes Page

Master 17

Objects

Backgrounds 32

Organisation Charts 44

Tables 48

Organisation Charts

Creating 44

Formatting 46

Package for CD 123

Paragraph Spacing 15

Pictures
- Inserting from File 38

Presentation
- Perfecting 115
- Printing 121

Printing
- Handouts 122
- Notes Pages 122
- Slides 121

Publishing
- To the Web 125

Reviewing 117
- Compare and Merge 119

Slide
- Design 25
- Hiding 79
- Inserting 77
- Master 12
- Setup 25
- Start and End 113
- Summary 114
- Transitions 90

Slide Show
- Custom 80
- Setting Up 95
- Timings 93
- Transitions 90

Sounds
- File Types 63
- Inserting 63

Speaker's Notes
- Adding 112

Spell Checking 115

Styles 11

Table
- Inserting 48

Template
- Creating 22
- Using 23

Text
- Boxes 31

Timings
- Applying 93

Transitions 90

Video Editing 67

WordArt
- Inserting 34

Other Products from CiA Training

CiA Training is a leading publishing company, which has consistently delivered the highest quality products since 1985. A wide range of flexible and easy to use self teach resources has been developed by CiA's experienced publishing team to aid the learning process. These include the following materials at the time of publication of this product:

- **Open Learning Guides**
- **ECDL/ICDL & ECDL/ICDL Advanced (ECDL Foundation Qualification)**
- **New CLAIT, CLAIT Plus & CLAIT Advanced (OCR Qualification)**
- **CiA Revision Series**
- **ITQs (Industry Standard Qualification)**
- **e-Citizen (ECDL Foundation Qualification)**
- **Trainer's Packs with iCourse**
- **Start IT (City & Guilds Qualification)**
- **Skill for Life in ICT (Industry Standard Qualification)**
- **iCourse - Course customising software**

We hope you have enjoyed using our materials and would love to hear your opinions about them. If you'd like to give us some feedback, please go to:

www.ciatraining.co.uk/feedback.php

and let us know what you think.

New products are constantly being developed. For up to the minute information on our products, to view our full range, to find out more, or to be added to our mailing list, visit:

www.ciatraining.co.uk